SERVING ON
THE BIG SHIPS

Bon voyage at New York to the illustrious *Queen Mary*. (*Author's Collection*)

SERVING ON THE BIG SHIPS
LIFE ON THE LINERS

WILLIAM H. MILLER

FONTHILL

This book is dedicated with affection and respect
to all the ships at sea, to their architects
and builders, and to the men women who take them
and us around the world

Cover: Painting by Robert Lloyd.

Fonthill Media Language Policy

Fonthill Media publishes in the international English language market. One language edition is published worldwide. As there are minor differences in spelling and presentation, especially with regard to American English and British English, a policy is necessary to define which form of English to use. The Fonthill Policy is to use the form of English native to the author. William H. Miller was born and educated in the USA; therefore American English has been adopted in this publication.

Fonthill Media Limited
Fonthill Media LLC
www.fonthill.media
office@fonthillmedia.com

First published in the United Kingdom and the United States of America 2024

British Library Cataloguing in Publication Data:
A catalogue record for this book is available from the British Library

Typeset in Mrs Eaves XL Serif Narrow
Printed and bound in England

Contents

Foreword

For me, life at sea, working on ships, has been wonderful. Growing up outside Manchester and surviving the dark, austere days of World War II, my very first time outside the UK was over seventy years ago, back in 1950. I was eighteen, in the army, and stationed in Austria. That posting ignited my interest in travel, to see the world, visit new places.

Before the army, I had worked for the Manchester Ship Canal in their head offices. When I returned, I was rehired, but to the harbormaster's office in the Salford Docks. I would see all the ships, coming and going, and wondered where they had been and where they were headed. At lunchtime, I wandered along the docks, saw the ships at berth, and even visited some of them. My curiosity about ships and travel was peaked further.

Later, I wrote to several shipping lines, and Royal Mail Lines was the first to reply. I was summoned to London, interviewed, and soon hired. I became the ship's clerk (and later promoted to assistant purser and then full purser). My first ship was an elderly freighter, the *Gascony*, which then was the second oldest in the Royal Mail fleet and managed to survive the war.

I had a little cabin just aft of the funnel. I earned 3 or 4 pounds a week. The *Gascony* was very, very slow and made only about 10 knots at best. She just crept, it seemed. On one voyage I recall it took us three weeks to go from Kingston, Jamaica, to London. We carried sugar and lots of rum.

I later served on Royal Mail's luxurious flagship *Andes* and then joined the Furness-Bermuda Line and served on their *Ocean Monarch*. My interest in travel continued and grew steadily—and ships were the "vessels" to travel, to see the world. And life at sea is interesting and rewarding, especially on passenger ships where you could meet all sorts of people.

I have been very fortunate to have had a life of travel, much of it in ships. I am therefore happy to write this foreword to Bill Miller's latest book of recollections of staff and owners of so many ships.

Des Kirkpatrick
New York City
Winter 2023

Acknowledgments

Creating a book is like manning a ship—it takes many hands. As the author, I might be the equal to the chief purser. I develop a title, gather materials, and then create. With that, many thanks to Fonthill Media, to Alan Sutton, Jay Slater, and staff, for taking on this project. Secondly, great thanks to Robert Lloyd for another superb cover and to Des Kirkpatrick for his fine foreword. And added first-class thanks to Michael Hadgis, Anthony La Forgia, and Tim Noble. Added thanks to Captain James McNamara and Captain Justin Zizes.

Further thanks to David Andrews, the late Frank Andrews, Tony Bannon, the late Bill Barber, Barrie Beavis, Trevor Blackwell, Cato Christensen, Terence Clarkson, Tony Costello, Giuseppe Covcurullo, Anna D'Ambrosio, the late Robert Cummins, Geoff Edwards, Jim Eldridge, Nick Evans, Ron Evans, the late David Fitzgerald, Alan Gilchrist, Robert Gordon, Terry Hopley, Alan Hulse, Herbert Jager, the late Brenton Jenkins, John Jones, the late Norman Knebel, Robert Leslie, John Malone, Mike McDougle, Gordon McKay, George Munn, the late Robert Pelletier, Scott Peterson, Peter Plowman, Henry Poulton, the late S. W. Rawlings, Maureen Ryan, Rick Spath, Robert Stanhope, Arthur Taylor, and Leonard Weir. Companies and organizations which are due thanks include British India Line, Crystal Cruises, Cunard Line, P&O, Port Authority of New York & New Jersey, Port Authority of the Port of Port Everglades, Silversea Cruises, Steamship Historical Society of America, Union-Castle Line, Viking Ocean Cruises, and World Ship Society, Port of New York Branch.

Introduction

have been traveling on passenger ships for some sixty years, and lecturing aboard them for over forty years. Yes, being aboard ships is quite wonderful. And, of course, so is visiting faraway places! As a speaker, I have met and often interviewed many fascinating people, most especially former ships' staff: captains, engineers, stewards, waiters, those suited elevator boys. Each of them has cherished memories—some very plentiful and highly detailed. This book reveals their stories of life on the liners, including in some of the greatest of ships, such as the Cunard Queens, the *United States*, and the *France*, but also in some of the more remote, perhaps less-remembered ships belonging to the likes of the British India and Blue Funnel lines. Of course, it is interesting to hear of, say, Elizabeth Taylor on board the *Queen Elizabeth* and the duke and duchess of Windsor on the *United States*, but it is also evocative to hear of a maharaja on the Anchor Line and tea traders on British India.

This book is a collection of interviews, remembrances, and tales from countless voyages and countless meetings with people who served on the big ships. Yes, it was life on the liners.

Bill Miller
Secaucus, New Jersey
Winter 2023

1

The Cunard Queens in the 1960s: Maureen Ryan

Maureen Ryan, who, in 1963, began as a stenographer in the purser's office aboard those giant ships, recalled: "In the early 1960s, Cunard's *Queen Mary* and *Queen Elizabeth* still had the true aura of the 1930s. These were ships of different architecture." The 81,000-grt *Mary* and the 83,000-grt *Elizabeth* still spent much of the year making five-day crossings between New York, Cherbourg, and Southampton. One of them sailed from Manhattan's "Luxury Liner Row" almost every Wednesday, arriving in England on the following Monday evening. Fares for first class started at $400, cabin class at $250, and tourist at $175. Those 28½-knot super liners had huge reputations, including heroic records from trooping service in World War II before, beginning in 1946–47, going on to become the most successful pair of big liners ever to sail the Atlantic. In war, they had safely transported over 15,000 troops per voyage; in peace, with far greater comfort, the 1,018-foot-long *Queen Mary* carried 1,957 passengers in three classes while the 1,031-foot-long *Queen Elizabeth* had a maximum of 2,233 berths.

"You lived and breathed class on those ships," remembered Ms. Ryan. "The three classes were like separate cities. As part of the crew, there were very high standards in every way at Cunard: behavior, dress and especially discipline. But Cunard was also a warm and friendly company, which, I suspect, was because of the great American influence. I had worked previously for P&O, on board their *Chusan*, which by comparison was cold, reserved, very snobbish. Cunard had more regional management and was more relaxed in many ways. The passengers were more important at Cunard whereas the officers and top staff seemed to be superior, and act superior, at P&O."

"Many Cunard crewmembers lived either in or around Southampton in those days," added Ms. Ryan. "Some could trace generations working for Cunard and were very proud of their service, their continued service, with such a great company. But there were rules, in fact very strict rules. For example, no crewmembers, not even captains, could have guests aboard back then. We had all sorts of staff back then. There were bankers in the ship's banks, for example, who not only had to be skilled, but also single and socially adept. There was even a separate bank in each class. We also had impeccable bellboys, who looked angelic and sweet, but often who were really little terrors. They were actually very worldly wise. It was all charm for tips!"

Maureen Ryan added, "The shop staff worked in a shopping arcade we called Regent Street on board the *Queen Mary*. The lady assistant pursers wore WREN-like uniforms, which many of them remembered from the days of World War II. The purser's office used to close at noon and then did not reopen until 2:30. There were these great drinks parties in between. In the purser's office, we prepared those massive passenger lists, which included full name, title and home city. Then we would create an errata edition with corrections and then an addendum edition. It all had to be perfectly done, with immense attention to detail. And, of course, every title had to be correct."

"We had a very busy mail room on board each ship," she added. "Then passengers still wrote lots of letters and cards. We also provided steno and typing services, at a cost, of course. And the butchers looked after the dogs. We still had elevator attendants, who called out each and every deck by name. They were often disabled seamen from World War II, possibly missing an arm, but whom Cunard looked after. They also helped part-time in the libraries."

"I am still in touch with some of the crew from those halcyon days on the old *Queen Mary* and *Queen Elizabeth*," concluded Ms. Ryan. "They were great ships, the great 'monsters' of the Atlantic. But sadly, it is a way of life gone forever."

Maureen Ryan served with Cunard for over forty years and was later assigned, in 1968, to the *Queen Elizabeth 2* and then, in 2003, to the *Queen Mary 2*.

Above left: "Getting there is half the fun"—Cunard's iconic slogan for transatlantic crossings. (*Author's Collection*)

Above right: Tourist-class baggage for five nights between New York and Southampton. (*Author's Collection*)

The magnificent *Queen Elizabeth*, the world's largest liner, outbound at Southampton. (*ALF Collection*)

Above: Sailing from the Ocean Terminal at Southampton. (*Cunard Line*)

Right: The *Queen Elizabeth* resting between voyages at New York's Pier 90. (*ALF Collection*)

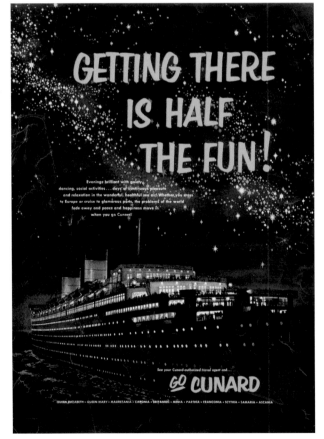

Above: On a summer's afternoon, another departure by the *Queen Elizabeth* from Southampton. (*ALF Collection*)

Left: Romantic and enchanting nights crossing the North Atlantic. (*Cunard Line*)

Opposite above: The last three-stacker: The beloved *Queen Mary* departing from Southampton. (*Author's Collection*)

Opposite below left: Welcome to New York—the 81,237-ton *Queen Mary* waits in New York's Lower Bay. (*Author's Collection*)

Opposite below right: The 1,019-foot-long *Queen Mary* at sea and heading for New York at 28½ knots. (*ALF Collection*)

Above: Looking back! The *Queen Mary* during her maiden crossing in May 1936. (*ALF Collection*)

Left: Final visit: The 1,957-passenger *Queen Mary*'s final visit to New York in September 1967. (*Author's Collection*)

Above left: The *Queen Mary* at Southampton. (*Mick Lindsay Collection*)

Above right: Rare occasion: The *Queen Elizabeth* (left) and the *Queen Mary* together at New York's Pier 90 in a view dated December 1948. (*Cunard Line*)

Below: Last night: The *Queen Mary*'s final visit to New York in September 1967. (*Author's Collection*)

2
Working the Liners from Down Under: Robert Cummins

As a young boy of twelve, Robert Cummins would bicycle to South Head, in the outer harbor of Sydney, Australia, and stare in great fascination as huge North Atlantic liners like the *Queen Mary*, *Queen Elizabeth*, *Île de France*, *Mauretania*, *Aquitania*, and *Nieuw Amsterdam* sailed off and then over the horizon. The year was 1940. Those gray-painted ships were being sent to far-off Ceylon, Bombay, and Suez with troops. Young Robert thought, "Wouldn't it be great to have a job on one of those ships." His wish and desire came true. In 1984, when we met aboard P&O's *Sea Princess*, he was in his thirty-seventh year at sea, having served on a wide variety of passenger ships, including some of the finest. Many of these ships sailed in the pre-jet age, when passengers were often divided by class and were being conveyed from "A" to "B."

Bob Cummins has served as a restaurant waiter, drinks steward, bedroom steward, pantryman, crew attendant, deck steward, and even as a captain's tiger (the master's steward and valet). In 1948, soon after World War II ended and shipping returned to normal commercial business, he began to implement his notion to see the world. "I was hired as a second-class waiter on the *Aorangi*, a beautiful old ship dating from 1924 and which had once been the biggest motor liner in the world. She had grand style: a domed reading and writing room, a big Steinway in the music room and an observation gallery on the upper deck, which surrounded the first-class restaurant and with cabins facing onto this. We sailed between Sydney, Auckland, Fiji, Honolulu, Victoria, and Vancouver. There was a five-day turnaround at Vancouver, and I can well recall paying a nickel to cross the Lion's Gate Bridge as a walking pedestrian. I spent my twenty-first birthday beneath the Aloha Tower in Honolulu, when there were only rice fields between the docks and the downtown city. We had a two-week turnaround at Sydney, which meant ten days off and four days' work. This seems incredible in this age, where containerships rarely spend more than twenty-four to forty-eight hours in port or where major cruise ships are in and out in ten to twelve hours. On the 17,000-ton *Aorangi*, along with 212 in first class and 170 in second class, we also carried 104 in third class or steerage and all at very low fares. We sailed alongside an American troopship, the *Marine Trooper*, which was taking war brides and other low-fare passengers from Sydney up to San Francisco. On the *Aorangi*, we carried lots of American and Australian ex-servicemen as well. I especially recall one young lady, who was to marry an Argentine sailor. She traveled with us to Vancouver, then took Greyhound across America and then Moore McCormack's *Brazil* down to Buenos Aires from New York. It was not as simple as today's connecting airline flights.

"The *Aorangi* was owned by the Union Steamship Company of New Zealand, which was part of the enormous P&O group of companies. In 1954, P&O itself decided to expand their liner service from the South Pacific to North America. Their *Oronsay* had been sent up to California and British Columbia and was a blazing success. The old *Aorangi* was suddenly out of work. She was sent home to Scotland, where she was built, and scrapped."

Bob next joined a string of Australian intercoastal liners, small but smart passenger ships that were in fact in their twilight years. "In 1950, I signed-up with the now defunct Adelaide Steamship Company. I was assigned to the 9,100-ton *Manunda*, which plied two routes. During the Australian summer, she sailed between Sydney, Melbourne, Adelaide, and Fremantle; then in winter, she went off on one-class cruises of seventeen to twenty-one days out of Sydney to Brisbane, the Great Barrier Reef, Townsville, and Cairns. She was a very handsome ship, one of the stock motor liners produced by British shipbuilders in the 1930s. Among these coastal liners, there were really only slight differences and modifications between them, those special modifications that suited their specific owners.

"I was next assigned to the *Manoora*, also for the Adelaide Steamship Company. At nearly 11,000 tons and with space for 360 passengers in two classes, she worked the same coastal route as the *Manunda*. In the end, she was sold to Indonesia's President Sukarno and became the pilgrim ship *Ambulombo*. Afterward, I went to the *Kanimbla*, the best of these ships and the queen of the Australian coastal liner fleet. Built in 1936, she was beautifully appointed, superbly maintained, highly reputed, in short a pocket version of the beautiful *Nieuw Amsterdam*. Her crew stayed with her and almost always remained the same. There was tremendous attachment and loyalty to the *Kanimbla*. Apart from the Sydney-Fremantle service, she ran about six annual thirty-day cruises that were very, very popular and always fully booked. We'd sail from Sydney to Port Moresby, Manila, Yokohama, Kobe and then return."

The 8,100-ton *Westralia* of Huddart Parker Limited was Bob Cummins' next post. "In the early fifties, she was already an old ship and with grand style, but with a special duty: trooping

The veteran Pacific liner *Aorangi*. (*Author's Collection*)

The Australian coastal liner *Duntroon*. (*Peter Plowman Collection*)

Above : Built in 1936, the 11,000-ton *Kanimbla* was considered by many to be the finest of the Australian coastal passenger ships. (*Peter Plowman Collection*)

Left: In her later years, the 484-foot-long *Kanimbla* sailed as the Japanese-owned *Oriental Queen*. Seen at Sydney, note the *Southern Cross* is berthed behind. (*Peter Plowman Collection*)

Another view of the all-white *Oriental Queen*, seen while cruising in the South Pacific. (*Author's Collection*)

The *Manoora* could carry up to 360 passengers—260 in first class and 100 in second class. (*Peter Plowman Collection*)

The flat-stacked *Wanganella* maintained service between Australia and New Zealand and carried some 425 passengers in two classes. (*Peter Plowman Collection*)

between Alexandria and Trieste for the British government. Soon afterward, I was again transferred, this time to the 9,500-ton *Wanganella*, a twin-stack motor liner that was the flagship of Huddart Parker. Fondly known as 'the *Wanga*,' we sailed one week between Sydney and Auckland, and the next week between Sydney and Wellington. Our passengers were mixed: Australians and New Zealanders. Entering Wellington harbor was always perilous, however, as a ship went on to the local rocks once every five years. We didn't want to be one of that lot. Another nice, well-kept ship, she was like all the others—*Manunda, Manoora*, and *Kanimbla*—in that they ran themselves. They were like marvelous, precision clocks. As staff, we just looked after them."

Bob went next to the Burns Philip Line, a huge Australian shipping firm and agency that literally "owned" the South Pacific back then. "I was put aboard the Company's largest passenger ship, the 6,200-ton, 180-passenger *Bulolo*. She did an island run—from Sydney, Brisbane, and sometimes Townsville to Honiara, the Solomon Islands, Port Moresby, and Rabaul. Used as Lord Mountbatten's command ship during World War II, harbors such as Port Moresby were still littered with wartime wrecks in the mid-'50s. Our captain was a great character. He had tanks and tubs surrounding his bridge and which were used for the tropical fish and reptiles he was bringing down to the Sydney Zoo. Also known as 'Mad Bill' to us, he treated the 15-knot *Bulolo* like a speedboat and took great delight in high-speed encounters and maneuvers. We carried traders, merchants, civil servants, and some tourists, but all with one difficulty: the little *Bulolo* was very, very hot. There was no air-conditioning. On board, she was an absolute sweatbox.

"My next ship was also my last Australian liner, the *Duntroon*, built in 1936 and of 10,300 tons. Named after the Duntroon Military Academy, she shared the Sydney coastwise service with the *Kanimbla, Manoora*, and others, and this group thereby provided a weekly sailing in each direction. While we also did the occasional cruise out of Sydney to Fiji, Noumea, and New Caledonia, we had special duty: taking occupation forces from Australia to Japan. We usually put into Yokohama. Unfortunately, by the early '60s, these ships were killed-off by Australian industrial trouble, by disputes with the dockers as well as the sailors. To their owners, they simply became too expensive and too troublesome. Their endings were rather harsh. They would be abruptly laid-up at some buoy in Sydney harbor and then, quite suddenly, vanish—and often with a Chinese crew. Almost the entire Australian coastal passenger fleet collapsed and then disappeared."

In 1960, Bob Cummins looked to overseas service and made the rounds of the big British shipping offices in downtown Sydney. In quick time, he joined the well-known Shaw Savill Line of London. "I was given a 'working passage,' a one-way run in the freighter *Cymric*. Loaded with general cargo, meats, and wool, we set off on the long voyage to Britain. At one point, for twenty-three days, we seemed to 'vanish' off the face of the earth, sailing from Invercargill in New Zealand direct to Balboa in the Panama Canal Zone. From there, we crossed to Dunkirk and then to Hull, Glasgow, Liverpool, and finally London. I have lived in London ever since."

Since Shaw Savill was part of the huge Furness Withy Group, Bob soon transferred to that firm's affiliate passenger ship division. He was assigned to the Royal Mail Lines and their 20,300-ton *Amazon*. "Then a brand-new beauty, she had the finest first-class restaurant I've ever seen and which sat all of 100 or so of the first-class passengers at a single seating. We'd have older English diplomats, the Argentine land barons and aristocracy, wealthy British tourists and some well-heeled wintertime round-trippers. There was also a second class with eighty-two berths and 275 in third class, but which was primarily for Spanish and Portugese immigrants bound for South America. They would board at Vigo and at Lisbon. We trained the British passengers down to the Tilbury Landing Stage from London (after a ten-day stay for cargo handling in the Royal Docks) and then had a short tender call at Boulogne. In South America, we called at Rio, Santos, Montevideo, and then offloaded all final passengers at Buenos Aires. The ship was then moved, for five days, to La Plata to load Argentine beef. We would then return to Buenos Aires, take on passengers and then sail in reverse homeward to the U.K. Unfortunately, British industrial problems killed these ships [the other sisters being the *Aragon* and *Arlanza*]. Often, we would return to South America with half the cargo we brought up because of some dockers' dispute on the London Docks. Three-class ships with sizeable freezer cargo spaces and in the increasingly cost-sensitive '60s, these three liners never quite made it. Even later, in less than ten years, when they transferred over to Shaw Savill [the *Amazon* became the *Akaroa*], they were equally unsuccessful."

Bob Cummins joined the still-large P&O-Orient Lines in 1966, just after the devastating and decisive British maritime strike (in May–June), which alone saw twenty-five liners idle at Southampton and which signaled the downfall and then decline of the last big British passenger fleet. "I spent two years on the *Orcades* and did six trips around the world in her. We were carrying diverse passengers—from the titled rich in first class to immigrants in tourist class. In first class, many passengers bought expensive tickets; down in tourist, they were often going out to Australia on the ten-pound, fare-assisted scheme. Outbound, we were always 'chocker-block.' I was aboard the *Orcades* a year later when the Suez Canal was suddenly and very dramatically closed. We were outward bound in the Mediterranean, steaming from London to Port Said. The captain was cabled to return to Gibraltar and await further instructions. The mood on board grew uneasy and unsure. Finally, we were ordered to proceed via the Atlantic—to Dakar, then Cape Town and Durban and then onward to Bombay, Colombo, Singapore, Fremantle, Adelaide, Melbourne, and Sydney. The ship's schedule was in chaos—our regular four-week sailing became a seven-week voyage."

Bob continued on P&O's "big white liners." "Thereafter, I did fifteen 'line voyages' in the Company flagship *Canberra*. Included was a seven-week Pacific Circle cruise that included Vancouver, San Francisco, Los Angeles, and Acapulco. Going out on the regular runs to Australia from Southampton, we traveled by way of Dakar,

The 9,876-ton *Wanganella* departing from Sydney. (*Peter Plowman Collection*)

The *Wanganella* seen in her final days as an accommodation ship. (*Peter Plowman Collection*)

Above left: An imposing view of the Australian liner *Westralia*. (*Author's Collection*)

Above right: The *Bulolo* operated between Australia and New Guinea and carried 180 passengers, all first class. (*Author's Collection*)

Papua New Guinea issued a stamp honoring the 6,400-ton *Bulolo*. (*Author's Collection*)

P&O's *Canberra*, the largest liner ever built for the U.K.–Australia run, is seen at Auckland in this view dated 1984. (*Author's Collection*)

The 1948-built *Orcades* is seen at Melbourne. (*Bill Barber Collection*)

Freetown, Cape Town, and Durban and then sailed nine days direct to Fremantle. Every night after Cape Town, it seemed, we lost an hour in time and the staff were on their knees by Australia. It was exhausting. Once, we had 2,200 passengers on board and with over 500 children. Most unusually, we then had to have three sittings."

While Bob also served in P&O's *Orsova* and *Arcadia*, for both world voyages and cruising, he also had a stint of service in a rather unique, but short-lived P&O passenger operation. "The 11,600-ton passenger ferry *Eagle* was operated by Southern Ferries Ltd, a P&O Group firm, on six-day roundtrips sailing from Southampton to Lisbon and Tangier, and then returning via Lisbon. We could carry 750 passengers and as many as 200 cars and 100 trucks on two electrically controlled vehicle decks. I especially remember three huge storms that we encountered on this ship. The third was, however, the worst. Just as we came out of Tangier, we ran into a sinister Atlantic gale. Even big 200,000-ton supertankers took refuge at Lisbon, but we continued onward. We actually 'vanished,' without any contact for three days and three nights. No one could locate us. At one point, we were caught between 2,000-ton waves and our bow slipped under for thirty seconds. It was the longest thirty seconds of my life. Another gigantic wave pushed us over to 44 degrees, but we miraculously up-righted. The captain, who spent endless, near super-human hours on the bridge, was badly injured when a window was smashed and splintered. He was so heavily bandaged afterward that he looked like a mummy.

Finally, a deep-sea tug out of Falmouth found us, put a towline out and then attempted to put a special pilot aboard. Most unfortunately, just as he was attempting to board, another huge wave slammed down and the poor man was sliced in two."

"The *Eagle* was an interesting if unusual concept for P&O, but hard hit by the worldwide recession of 1974," added Bob Cummins. "She was finally finished-off by an industrial dispute. She became a financial loss and was sold to France's Paquet Lines to be renamed *Azur*."

Bob was also aboard P&O's 28,100-ton *Oronsay* during her final cruise from Sydney to Hong Kong in the summer of 1975. "Myself, I left with the passengers at Hong Kong and we were flown home to Australia. Then, with just a skeleton crew, the twenty-four-year-old liner made the twenty-four-hour passage over to Kaohsiung on Taiwan to meet her end. A big hole had been dug on the beach there and the ship was deliberately run aground. The last P&O staff members signed her over and then the scrappers went aboard."

Bob's last assignment was P&O Cruises' *Sea Princess*, the former *Kungsholm*. "She is a very beautiful ship, certainly one of the best afloat today [1984]," he concluded. "After her takeover by P&O in 1978, we had to go through a 're-teething' stage and had to work very hard. We had to make her more British, more P&O. She is a sweet ship—with a good atmosphere and a high degree of passenger loyalty."

Bob Cummins' original dream of a life at sea certainly came true.

Dressed in flags for cruising, the mighty 2,234-passenger *Canberra* is seen berthed at Funchal on Madeira in October 1980. (*Author's Collection*)

Above left: The 1,545-passenger *Orcades* is seen in the original corn-colored hull of the Orient Line. (*Mick Lindsay Collection*)

Above right: Loving care! Two Lascar seamen attend to the starboard anchor of the *Canberra*. (*Author's Collection*)

Above left: An iconic poster from P&O. (*Norman Knebel Collection*)

Above right: The very popular *Arcadia*, commissioned in 1954, is seen departing from Circular Quay at Sydney. (*Frank Andrews Collection*)

The 709-foot-long *Orcades* departing from Melbourne. (*Tim Noble Collection*)

At sea on board the *Orsova*. (*Tim Noble Collection*)

Togetherness: The *Oronsay* (left) and *Arcadia* berthed together at Yokohama. (*P&O*)

The *Sea Princess* berthed at Circular Quay, Sydney. (*Bill Barber Collection*)

3

Hotel Manager: Herbert Jager

Overseeing the day-to-day operations of a cruise ship is no easy task, especially if it is a high-end, luxury ship where it all moves like a floating palace. Crystal Cruises, gold-plated from stem to stern, known especially for its impeccable service and almost extraordinary staff and crew, is further blessed in having some of the finest hotel managers on all the seven seas. One of them is Herbert Jager. He is the ideal "right man in the right job." He has, for example, smooth, highly competent attention to detail, the ability to keep at his departments in nothing but the highest form, and, quite importantly, to also have time for the guests. Recently, on board the stunning *Crystal Symphony*, sailing the ink-blue waters of the sun-drenched Caribbean, the ship shined, flowed, worked to absolute perfection—all largely due to him. While we have sailed together many times before—aboard the *Crystal Harmony* (now the *Asuka II*, cruising for Crystal's Japanese parent, NYK Line) and on the newer *Crystal Serenity*—we were together again aboard the 790-foot-long *Crystal Symphony*, bound for beautiful Bermuda and the sunny Caribbean from New York.

A native of Salzburg, Austria, Herbert first went to sea back in 1981 aboard the 550-passenger *Royal Viking Sky*, one of the then-impeccable trio belonging to the five-star Royal Viking Line and said to offer the most luxurious cruising of its time. Previously, he had worked as a chef in Austrian winter resorts and for the United Nations, cooking for world leaders including President Giscard d'Estaing of France. Royal Viking was a great starting point, an idyllic training ground, for life on the high seas. "In 1981, when I started, Royal Viking and Norwegian America Line [with their *Sagafjord* and *Vistafjord*] were the only true luxury cruise ships of that time," said Herbert. "On Royal Viking, we sold only full world cruises. There were no segment passengers then, not until the late '80s in fact. We'd have, say, 450 full world cruise passengers and it was all very dressy, very formal and guests travelling with not just one, but several trunks. Royal Viking was a very unique product with a very special clientele. Omar Sharif would be aboard doing bridge and Cary Grant and his wife did the full 100-day trip. Bob Hope did his Christmas Show on board and Dolly Parton was one of the guests. Of course, the service and the food were pure perfection. We had a huge repeater following, all members

of the Skald Club, and very little turnover amongst the officers and crew. Flying the Norwegian flag, we always had Norwegian Night as part of the entertainment and mostly Scandinavian crew. There was great Scandinavian influence, with just one setting in the restaurant, and the passengers went to the dining room for breakfast, lunch, and dinner. There was no bistro, no alternative restaurant, not even a snack bar on deck. The passengers dressed for lunch! Everyone had a set table, with set waiters and assistant waiters at every meal. We offered great food, fine entertainment, and the then novelty of daytime enrichment with guest lecturers. We had passengers who stayed aboard for months at a time."

"But these days, Royal Viking could not compete," added Herbert. "But then, in the '80s, there was no real competition." In 1988, he was sent to Finland to help set up the brand-new *Royal Viking Sun*, but soon afterward, the emerging Crystal called. Quickly, he was off to Nagasaki in Japan for the outfitting of their first ship—the new, ultra-luxurious 49,000-ton *Crystal Harmony*. As executive sous chef, he helped create the ship's award-winning culinary program. Six years later, in 1995, he was back in Finland, helping with the outfitting of the brand-new, slightly larger, 51,000-ton *Crystal Symphony*. By then, he was also promoted to hotel director. Later, in 2003, he saw the 68,000-ton *Crystal Serenity* come into service. "I moved to the Crystal offices in Los Angeles in 2000, to start the planning for the *Serenity*," he added. "That took two years and then I spent a year at the shipyard, at St Nazaire in France, as the ship was constructed."

In 2006, Herbert also oversaw the extensive refit at a Norfolk, Virginia, shipyard for the *Crystal Symphony*. "The ship, then 11 years old, had a facelift," he added, "which included everything from new carpeting to restyled public rooms to improved staterooms."

Today, aboard the likes of the 950-bed *Symphony*, the high-end luxury cruise business is different, changing, even evolving. "The clientele is changing, of course," reflected Herbert. "Among other demands, today's cruise passengers want better value. They will spend the money but want value in return. There are different needs—such as specialty, gourmet coffees and teas, greater variety in foods and alternative dining, and greater entertainment. Now, daytime entertainment is as important as nighttime.

"Passengers know far more these days about food and wine, but also want to stay active, healthy and like mental nourishment as well. We must have spas, extensive spas, for example, these days. Thirty years ago, as a comparison, there were no gyms on the Royal Viking ships. We also have more families these days, especially in the summer months. We are also in the age of customized shore excursions. Guests want unique experiences and are willing to pay for them. They want something very special. There has been big change and great growth in shore excursions in, say, the past five years. For example, we offer customized tours in places like China and Italy, a ride in a Russian MiG fighter [said to cost $15,000 and so ranking as the priciest shore excursion anywhere], and other, unique excursions like a private yacht over to Capri and then back by private helicopter. There is also growing demand for our Vintage Room, which is very successful. In a private setting, twelve people pay a total of $2,100 for a long, leisurely meal with the best food and best wines."

On board the 21-knot *Crystal Symphony*, Herbert Jager's domain is, much like being the mayor of a small city, actually quite immense. He oversees five major departments aboard the gleaming, all-white *Symphony*—food and beverage, rooms division, contracted services (such as the spa, photo shop, and boutiques), entertainment, and finance and accounting. "We have to do not just the best, but the very best," he concluded. "We are unique in the cruise industry because we are a floating luxury resort, rather than just a ship with rooms."

The luxurious *Royal Viking Sky* berthed at Hamburg during a summer cruise. (*Author's Collection*)

Above left: The 539-passenger *Royal Viking Star* departing from New York's Pier 40 in October 1973. (*Author's Collection*)

Above right: The *Crystal Harmony* seen in Norwegian waters in 1993. (*Crystal Cruises*)

The 960-passenger *Crystal Symphony* is seen at Port Everglades. (*Port of Port Everglades Authority*)

The *Crystal Serenity* arrives and meets the *Crystal Symphony* in 2014. (*Author's Collection*)

4

The Smell of Curry:
Mike McDougle

could almost smell the curry! "They were said to be the best kept, most immaculate passenger ships using the port of Liverpool in the 1950s & '60s," said Mike McDougle, who served aboard Britain's long-gone Anchor Line and aboard the company's three 11,000-ton passenger ships, the *Caledonia*, *Cilicia*, and *Circassia*, which carried up to 300 one-class passengers each. "We were on the Indian run—sailing by way of Gibraltar, Port Said, and the Suez Canal to Karachi and, the final stop, to Bombay. We carried very few tourists actually, but mostly government people, lots of the old colonials, businessmen, tea merchants, and Indians including the occasional maharaja. Those Indian princes traveled with entire entourages that occupied as many as a dozen cabins on board. One royal, I think it was the Maharaja of Rawalpindi, had a stateroom just for his pet falcon."

"These Anchor liners were famed for their cuisine," added Mike. "They had all-Indian galley crews that prepared the most wonderful curries. Just having, say, lunch aboard at Liverpool was a treat. Anchor Line food was equal to the finest Indian restaurant. Anchor was also noted for its exceptional maintenance and shipboard care. Everything, even the engine room, was in pristine condition. Even though these ships were over twenty years of age, it was as if they'd just left the shipyard."

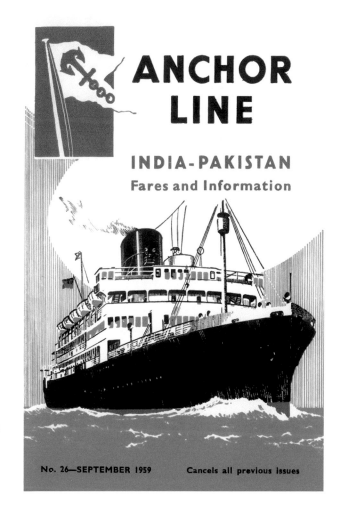

Right: Outward bound for India & Pakistan on the Anchor Line. (*Author's Collection*)

Below left: An evocative poster for Anchor Line's Middle Eastern services. (*Norman Knebel Collection*)

Below right: The inaugural booklet for the *Circassia* of 1937. (*Author's Collection*)

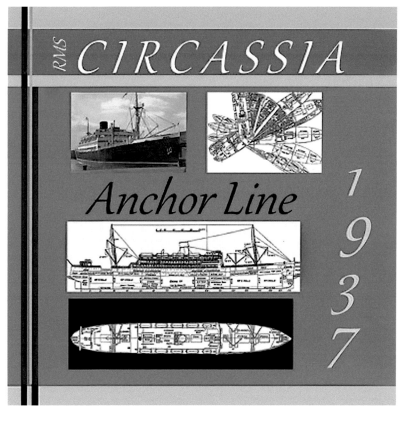

Above: The 300-passenger *Cilicia* berthed at Birkenhead. (*Mick Lindsay Collection*)

Left: The *Circassia* in dry dock at Liverpool. (*Mick Lindsay Collection*)

5

Sailing with Cunard:
Barrie Beavis

High luxury at sea: back in the 1950s, in the golden age of the great ocean liners, Cunard Line's *Caronia* was often said to be one of the most luxurious, if not the most luxurious liner afloat. She did almost nothing but long, luxurious, and very expensive cruises—around the world, the Mediterranean, and, in summer, to almost all of Scandinavia. Some 600 crew, many of them handpicked, looked after 600 passengers and so the service ratio was 1:1. A big liner in her own right, the *Caronia* was said to be like a big, floating country club—some passengers actually lived aboard for months at a time. One lady stayed for two years, another for three years, and one, the all-time champ of cruising, "lived" aboard for fourteen years! Painted in shades of green, the *Caronia* was dubbed the "Green Goddess"—and also called the "millionaires' yacht."

Barrie Beavis joined the great Cunard Company in 1958 and was promptly assigned to the *Caronia*. He was a junior engineer. "The *Caronia* was a plum assignment at Cunard in those days because she traveled just about all over the world. To the hotel staff, the stewards, and the waiters, she was much preferred over the other Cunarders, including the legendary *Queen Mary* and *Queen Elizabeth*, because the tips were so much greater. Fifteen-year-old bellboys were given 5- and 10-dollar tips just for opening a door. They did very well. At the dining room entrance, two of them stood at attention and greeted the guests. One would whisper a happy birthday to the other and, upon overhearing this, the passengers might hand him a $50 bill as a present. It was all a sham, of course."

"The longest cruises aboard the *Caronia* were the world cruises and some as long as 108 days," Barrie noted. "The *Caronia* was created especially as an 'export ship'—to bring US dollars into post-war Britain. The great majority of her passengers were older, richer Americans. These very wealthy passengers would come aboard in New York and stay for four months and sometimes longer. Sometimes, Cunard would redecorate their suites to their personal tastes. One lady liked African decor with leopard and zebra skins. The ship's photographer would photograph the suite first so it could later be returned to its original style and decor. I remember Miss McBeth, who stayed aboard for fourteen years, and traveled with a companion. She was rarely seen outside her suite, however. She was a great recluse. But occasionally, she might be seen on the promenade deck. On these long cruises, we would sometimes have long stays in port—three or four days in Cape Town, a week in India, four days in Hong Kong. We also had lots of overland tours—some passengers would leave the ship in, say, Bombay and not return until Singapore. Over the years, the crew made friends in the ports of call. Some created businesses—they'd buy jewels in, say, Rio and then sell them in South Africa. They made great profits.

"More than aboard other Cunarders, life on the *Caronia* became a 'way of life.' The ship's barber actually owned the beauty concessions and when he died, he left behind not just a few, but a whole street of houses in Liverpool. The chief steward made so much money he was picked-up by a Rolls-Royce at Southampton, while the captain went off in a Morris Miner. All tips actually went backwards, of course—waiters had to tip their assistants and then the cooks and assistant cooks in the galley. The same was true with stewards who in turn tipped the chief stewards and assistant chiefs. There was a kind of protocol to it all. There were also scams. In the bars, the barmen often bought cheap Champagne in New York and then sold it as Moët. If uncovered, they would be at the ready—'Sorry, sir, but I must have grabbed the wrong bottle!' Of course, there was theft as well—the stealing of food and meats in particular. Indeed, it was often said that Cunard could have built a third Queen with the amount that was stolen. But no one ever told on anyone—it was all discreet, with high secrecy and, of course, a fear of the Internal Revenue in the UK."

Barrie was paid $200 a month as a junior engineer aboard the *Caronia* in 1958. Beer was 10 pence a pint in the crew bar. "As an officer, we could eat with the passengers and host a table. We were not allowed, however, to order caviar or have strawberries," he recalled. "We did four hours on and eight hours off—and had double watches in thick fog. We had lots of characters among the crew, of course—and lots of old timers who had served in the war. One captain actually had an intense hatred of the Japanese from World War II. Once at Yokohama, as we were departing, he ordered the Japanese pilot off the ship, took full command himself, but then proceeded to ram the harbor breakwater and push a lighthouse into the sea. We had to return and stay for long, expensive repairs. [The *Caronia*'s bow was actually reshaped at the waterline during these repairs and altogether it made the ship a knot faster from then on.] Many crew spent all their wages during that extended stay and were broke for the rest of that world cruise. Another

The splendid *Caronia* berthed at Wellington, New Zealand, during a South Pacific–Far East cruise. (*Author's Collection*)

Dressed in flags and preparing to sail, the 932-passenger *Caronia* carried only up to 600 on her long, luxurious cruises. (*ALF Collection*)

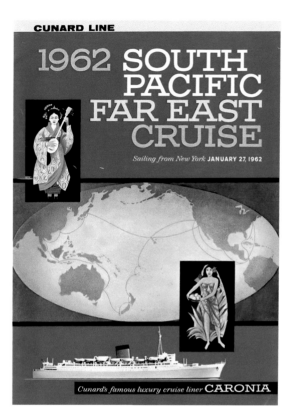

Above left: A hundred or so days and around the world on the impeccable *Caronia*. (*Author's Collection*)

Above right: Passengers came year after year on the *Caronia*'s long cruises. (*Author's Collection*)

Below: Arrival at Southampton for the 715-foot-long *Caronia*. (*ALF Collection*)

The *Queen Mary* (left) and *Caronia* berthed at Pier 90, New York—and with the bow of the *Flandre* approaching on the far right. (*Author's Collection*)

At the end of her days, the *Caronia* loitered around New York harbor as the financially troubled *Caribia*. (*Author's Collection*)

was a chief engineer, who was very mean and a great alcoholic. Once, when highly irritated, he went to the bridge and smashed the engine telegraph with an ax. I remember he'd also spend the day talking to the gin bottle he was going to finish that night. He feared no one aboard except the rigid superintendents then in our Liverpool headquarters. We also had some great characters, even eccentrics, among the crew. One steward bought a little monkey while we were in India, then collared it and walked it along the crew alleyways. He was eventually found out, ordered to throw it over the side, but sold it instead to a passenger, who kept it in the ship's kennel."

Many of the crew could not quite leave Cunard and the liners—it was their life, their entire life. "Many of the 'boys' lived for the sea and for the liners and for the glamour days," he added. "We had one captain who died immediately after his ship was retired. Some crew members went ashore to work in pubs and hotels, but many just faded away. Some actually died in tragic circumstances—alone, living on very limited means or sometimes penniless, in dreary accommodations in third-rate boarding houses."

"The *Caronia* was kept in mint condition for all of her Cunard years," concluded Barrie Beavis. "Her teak decks were white and we were always chipping away at rust and painting. Her green hull and upper decks were immaculate. Of course, every year we did a turn up in Liverpool in the Gladstone Dry Dock. There were repairs, general house cleaning and a massive fumigation—we had to rid even the ultra-luxurious *Caronia* of cockroaches!"

6
Purser Aboard the Great *France*: Terence Clark

As we approached the Panama Canal over forty years later, Terence Clark said: "Looking back, sailing for six years [1968–74] as a staff member aboard the liner *France* was one of the greatest times of my life." Together, we were aboard a current cruise ship, the *Crystal Serenity*. Born in Madagascar (to French parents), but then moving to France, he wanted to travel and so applied to the famed French Line, the Compagnie Generale Transatlantique, at their Paris offices. He was quickly hired, initially serving as a steward. He advanced quickly, however, and soon was promoted to the rank of assistant purser. He had a great asset: while he later changed his name to Terence Clark, he was then called Thierry and spoke five languages.

He recalled, "In the beginning, I was assigned to room service. I earned $500 a month [1968] and had three months' vacation each year. But as an assistant purser, I had different, varied duties. I welcomed Salvador Dali and his wife Gala aboard in their three adjoining suites. Dali brought along his two baby lions, which lived in one suite. The carpet had been specially removed and the lions were served boiled eggs in separate bowls. I also looked after lots of movie stars—like Lauren Bacall, Catherine Deneuve, and Marcello Mastroianni. I well recall the personal maids coming to the purser's office each evening to collect the jewelry for madam to wear. Everything had to be documented and recorded in great detail—and of course later returned and documented again. There were passengers who sailed, even on the five-day crossings between New York, Southampton, and Le Havre, with as much as $1 million in jewels. Overall, it was all very interesting work, but included long days and lots of compromise, understanding, and patience. Some passengers could be very demanding, even very difficult. On one crossing, we had a rather frightening moment. At 7 in the morning, Madame de Gaulle and her bodyguard were trapped—for twenty minutes—in an elevator. We had to notify the captain, who was not pleased. I had to relay information to Madame de Gaulle that 'help is on the way'."

The *France* made two highly publicized around-the-world cruises—in 1972 and 1974. "I have great memories of the '72 cruise. It was themed to the 100th birthday of Jules Verne and his *Around the World in 80 Days*," recalled Terry. "Some passengers booked several, inter-connecting suites and brought along their own servants. Others saved for a lifetime, even mortgaged their houses, to make the trip. I recall we could not land passengers at Easter Island because of heavy seas, but I was allowed to go ashore with the local officials. On this trip, it will be my first visit to Easter Island in forty-three years."

"Working aboard the *France* was like being in the army," added Terry. "There were inspections every day—and everything had to be perfect. There was a great hierarchy. It was all very French. One captain was not very social, but distant, removed, very stuffy. We rarely ever saw him. The head chef was, in ways, more important than the captain on board the *France*. Food and its preparation were very, very important at the French Line. Fortunately, the chef and I became good friends and so, rather than eating in the crew mess, I had lobster and caviar, the finest of everything. The unions on board were very powerful, of course. About 20 percent of us were non-union and often we were socially boycotted. In the end, of course, the unions killed the ship [1974]. There had been lots of strikes and work slowdowns, and more than once I had to temporarily serve in a dining room restaurant. Many of us saw the end coming even two years before. The writing was on the wall. In the end, a simple memo was sent out to all—it was the end for the *SS France*!" Terry quit his job months before the final voyage, leaving France and moving to Canada.

"The crew aboard the *France* felt they were lucky to have jobs, but were not especially proud of the ship itself. They were always complaining, even to the smallest detail such as the quality of the mineral water in the mess rooms. In the final years, even months, they did not see the light. Many of us made great tips in addition to our salaries. We were even generously, often very generously, tipped just to arrange bon voyage parties. We'd also fetch the dogs from the kennel, deliver messages, and, in high discretion, arrange secret rendezvous between passengers. We'd always know of an empty cabin or even suite. Along with the celebrities, we carried lots of government officials, friends of the French Line and their friends and families. Myself, I bought my first car just on tips."

These days, the *France* and the great French Line are memories, glorious memories mostly. "I saw the *France* as the *Norway*," concluded Terry, "but was surprised—it was no longer the same ship. When the *France* was retired, all the crew lost their jobs. I am still a member of the *SS France* Association and there are still news and stories and secrets from those good, old days."

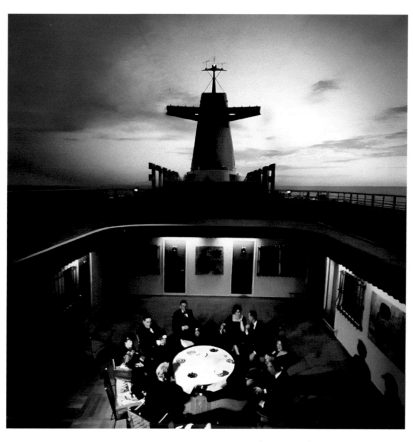

Above left: The 1,035-foot-long *France* was the world's longest liner when first commissioned in 1962. (*French Line*)

Above right: The top-deck courtyard for some first-class guests aboard the 2,044-passenger *France*. (*Author's Collection*)

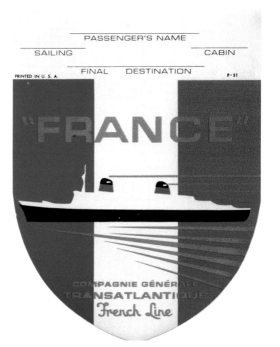

Above left: Five-night crossings between New York, Southampton, and Le Havre. (*Author's Collection*)

Above right: Tourist-class fares on board the France began at $200 in 1965. (*Author's Collection*)

Above: Winter morning: The *Atlantic* (top), *United States*, *France*, and *Queen Mary* at New York in February 1965. (*Port Authority of New York & New Jersey*)

Below left: A menu cover for gourmet dining on the *France*. (*Author's Collection*)

Below right: French artist Albert Brenet's superb depiction of the *France* arriving at Pier 88, New York. (*Moran Towing & Transportation Co.*)

7

Remembering the *Ellinis*: Leonard Weir

The Greek-flag Chandris Lines, which became Celebrity Cruises by 1990, was busily buying secondhand passenger ships in the 1960s. It seems they preferred both American and British tonnage, and this included the famed Matson liner *Lurline*, built in 1931 and very popular from her days on the San Francisco–Los Angeles–Honolulu run. While carrying up to 760 passengers in her Matson days, Chandris engineers had her refitted in 1963 for as many as 1,700 travelers. As the renamed *Ellinis*, she sailed mostly on the Europe–Australia and around-the-world routes, but also did cruising from Southampton, England, as well as Sydney, Australia.

After a stint on the London stage in *My Fair Lady*, Leonard Weir sailed from New Zealand all the way to London on board the 631-foot-long *Ellinis* in 1964. He remembered that all-white ship, and he was soon working for Chandris. "I was returning to England for summer stock and then returned for Australia for the Southern summer. Outgoing and rather personable, I was quickly made Entertainment Officer on the *Ellinis*. On the trips to England, we had lots of young Australians going to the UK and to Europe, and then returned with full loads of migrants. We collected the migrants at Bremerhaven, Rotterdam, Piraeus [for Athens], and even stopped at Dubrovnik to collect Yugoslavians. It was quite a multi-national passenger list," he remembered. "We were always choker-block. When the Suez Canal was closed, we sailed via South Africa, calling in at Cape Town. From there, it was ten days to Fremantle and then onward to Melbourne and Sydney."

Leonard Weir added, "We once hit a fierce storm, a Force 12. Waves towered above the ship for 10 whole days. All the kids were very sick and many adults too. We used to have three sittings for meals—one for children and then the first and second for adults. There was very little entertainment, but we offered Greek dance lessons. On the first night, we'd have a Greek cultural show, which was wonderful. We'd use lots of passengers as dancers, and they even threw plates and broke them. Even the captain joined in and threw plates. The ship was very friendly—and romance abounded; in fact, lots of Australian ladies later married Greek officers and crew."

While Leonard Weir went on to sail aboard the legendary *Queen Mary* and later with Costa Cruises, the *Ellinis* sailed on until 1980, when it was laid up; it was finally broken up in 1987.

Above: Flying the Greek colors, the *Britanis* was used on the Europe–Australia and around-the-world services. (*ALF Collection*)

Left: Chandris Lines became popular for reasonably priced cruises from England, Australia, and New York. (*Author's Collection*)

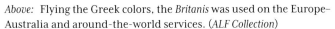

The *Ellinis* could carry over 1,600 passengers, all in tourist class. (*Bill Barber Collection*)

During a summer cruise, the *Britanis* meets with Italy's *Michelangelo*. (*Author's Collection*)

8

Serving on Penthouse Deck: Gordon McKay

Few shipboard staff can lay claim, at least in these times, to forty-three years with the same company. Gordon McKay is an exception. He joined the historic Cunard Line in 1961, when he first boarded the *Queen Mary*, the last of the celebrated three-stackers on the North Atlantic. He then went on to serve aboard the likes of the *Caronia, Mauretania, Sylvania, Queen Elizabeth*, and, beginning in late 1968, aboard the *Queen Elizabeth 2*. Before he retired in 2004, he was the most senior steward on Cunard.

"I will have done fifty years in service," he proudly noted in 2005. "Beginning at the age of fifteen, I did seven years in private service with the Guinness and Rothermere families. I used to rise at 5 in the morning and each day shine fifty pairs of shoes before joining a junior footman; together we would begin polishing the silver for the luncheon and dinner tables. I lived in a little room high up in a turret in a castle in Scotland. But I eventually wanted to travel, to see the world, and soon joined Cunard. I've stayed forty-three years."

"Those earlier Cunard liners, like the *Queen Mary* and *Queen Elizabeth*, were highly segregated ships. They were three class, and the divisions were rigidly enforced. Midships was first class and, of course, we had lots of celebrities on the crossings between Southampton, Cherbourg, and New York in the 1960s. I served Rosalind Russell, Bette Davis, Joan Bennett, Merle Oberon, and many, many aristocratic and wealthy people. There were many very rich people who traveled in grand style in those days. Some would come aboard with their own servants. One British couple sailed often, with their own valet and maid, and used the *Queens* to go between their homes in England and Bermuda. They would cross on either the *Mary* or the *Elizabeth* and then connect at New York with the *Queen of Bermuda*. They had a pattern: They would arrive on Tuesdays, spend four nights in New York, and then sail on Saturday afternoons aboard the *Queen of Bermuda*. We had separate cabins for servants that were adjacent to the passenger staterooms and suites aboard the *Queens*."

One of Gordon's favorite ships was Cunard's celebrated *Caronia*, the luxury liner that did almost nothing but long, expensive cruises and which was well known as the "Green Goddess." At 34,000 tons, she carried 600 crew for 600 or often fewer passengers. "I was with her for five years," he noted, "and she was then the happiest ship in the Cunard fleet. We had lots of repeaters, including passengers who stayed aboard for months at a time. I recall that it cost $40,000 for the ninety-five-day cruise around the world and for the best suite on board, Main Deck Number 39 and 40. I served Miss Clara MacBeth, who lived aboard for fourteen years and who traveled with a lady companion. Miss MacBeth had the same waiter year after year. She was quite a lovely lady, who kept all of her wits quite close to her hundredth birthday. I looked after her on the maiden voyage of the *QE2* in May 1969. She then occupied inter-connecting cabins 2065 and 2067, but passed away shortly afterward. No one has surpassed her to this day for continuous travel."

Gordon was aboard some sentimental voyages as well: The last cruise, a six-week trip around the Mediterranean out of New York, for the *Caronia* in October 1967 and the final crossing from New York to Southampton on board the *Queen Elizabeth* in October 1968. Immediately afterward, he was sent up to Scotland's River Clyde to join the nearly complete *QE2*. "I was part of the so-called 'advance party'," he said, "and looked after Prince Charles when he traveled with us for the first trip along the river, from Clydebank to Greenock. I prepared Cabin 1048 for the prince's day use and served breakfast to his personal detective. The prince was aboard from 7 in the morning until 3 that same afternoon. Years later, in the 1980s, I met Princess Diana and told her that I had served her husband. I almost met the queen herself when she came aboard for a pre-maiden voyage visit in May 1969, but missed her when her schedule fell behind and the royal routing on board was changed."

Gordon had been assigned to the *QE2*'s suites and penthouses up on Deck 8 since they were fitted on board in 1975. "I've looked after many guests, passengers like Lillian Gish, Cliff Richard, and Meryl Streep, over the years," he reported. "I was also aboard for the Falklands War in May 1982 when the *QE2* was used as a giant troopship. I looked after the commanding officers in the suites. It was interesting to see the truly brave and then the not-so-brave during that voyage. But it was not a time to be frightened."

In his final years, Gordon was still up by 4:30 and on duty by 7 a.m. He prepared cabin breakfasts, answered calls from the passengers, and later did cabin service. "I am one of only three original waiters left [2003] on board the *QE2*," he said proudly. "I still like the *QE2*. She is a very agreeable ship. The *Queen Mary 2* will be lovely as well, but very different. I will not be going to her, however. 2004 will be my last year with Cunard."

Indeed, Gordon McKay was unique.

Right: A Cunard sailing schedule issued in July 1959. (*Author's Collection*)

Below: The mighty *Queen Elizabeth* (left) meets the *Mauretania* in Southampton's Ocean Dock in this view dated 1963. (*ALF Collection*)

Above: Eastbound from New York to Cherbourg and then Southampton on board the *Queen Elizabeth*. (*Tim Noble Collection*)

Left: Early morning: The *Queen Mary* approaches New York from its Lower Bay. (*ALF Collection*)

Farewell and bon voyage for the *Queen Mary*! (*Author's Collection*)

The popular *Mauretania* took six days to sail between Southampton and New York. (*ALF Collection*)

Above left: Winter break: The 772-foot-long *Mauretania* is having her end-of-year overhaul at Liverpool in this view dated 1958. (*ALF Collection*)

Above right: Farewell to Pier 92 from the outbound *Queen Elizabeth*. (*Author's Collection*)

Above left: Crossing the North Atlantic—Cunard style! (*Cunard Line*)

Above right: Cunard passenger service to Montreal, Quebec, and Halifax. (*Norman Knebel Collection*)

Above: Building the *QE2* at Clydebank in Scotland. (*Cunard Line*)

Below: The *QE2*'s maiden arrival at New York in May 1969. (*Author's Collection*)

Another New York maiden arrival view for the 963-foot-long *QE2*. (*ALF Collection*)

At least four Moran tugs assist with the gala maiden arrival for the *QE2*. (*Moran Towing & Transportation Co.*)

Above left: The *QE2* was said to be the "most exciting" new liner of the early 1970s. (*Author's Collection*)

Above right: The mighty *QE2* at Adelaide in Australia in 2008. (*Bill Barber Collection*)

Departing from Port Hobart in Tasmania. (*Author's Collection*)

9

Purser Aboard the *United States*: David Fitzgerald

Dave Fitzgerald was a neighbor of mine, living in nearby Weehawken, New Jersey. He was also chief purser aboard the SS *United States,* sailing aboard that brilliant liner beginning with her maiden trip in July 1952 through to her very final voyage in November 1969.

He was precise, charming, and very good looking (and, in earlier days, was often used in United States Lines' publicity photos). In mid-life, he married one of his first-class passengers and together they lived happily thereafter in a roomy Tudor house in Weehawken, high above the Hudson—in fact, it was almost directly opposite Pier 86, at the foot of West 46th Street over in Manhattan. Pier 86 had been the regular berth for the 990-foot-long *United States,* but later, after being demolished, it became the permanent home to the aircraft museum USS *Intrepid.*

In later years, I visited Dave several times, often sitting together in his study in that big Weehawken house. He was quite an immaculately stylized man: blue blazers, always a shirt and tie, and Tartan slacks sometimes, and he drove a vintage Mercedes, which was always highly polished. Inside that roomy house, there were lots of keepsakes from his countless crossings to and from Europe.

In particular, the shelves were crammed, as I recall, with autographed photographs. Like soldiers in orderly formation, they were each handsomely framed—in silver from Tiffany, leather from Mark Cross, or in fancy blue and green enamel from London and Paris. There was an extraordinary list: the Eisenhowers, Herbert Hoover, Jimmy Stewart, Joan Crawford and Merle Oberon, Queen Frederika of Greece, the shah of Iran's sister, Lord Mountbatten, and, of course, the duke and duchess of Windsor. Expectedly, Dave had anecdotes about most of them: Joan Crawford scrubbing the floor of the bathroom in her suite, the queen of Greece having the ship's hairdresser on call three times a day, and the duchess of Windsor sitting down with him and very carefully planning a couple of luncheon parties (ladies only!) that were held in the sitting room of her main deck quarters (Dave told me that, back in the '50s, the duchess was not just curious but deeply interested in inviting an otherwise unknown passenger named Estée Lauder).

Dave was one of the last great links to the great *United States.* Dave's wife passed away in 2005 and Dave followed in 2016. By then, he was in his mid-nineties. The house has been sold, now gutted, and renovated. There were few heirs.

Right: The world's fastest liner, the *United States*, makes an early morning arrival at New York. (*Moran Towing & Transportation Co.*)

Below: Bunkering the 990-foot-long *United States* at Pier 86, New York. (*Author's Collection*)

Above left: Advertising from *Holiday* magazine in the 1950s. (*Author's Collection*)

Above right: In vivid ocean blue, a poster for the *United States*. (*Norman Knebel Collection*)

Outbound at Newport News, Virginia. (*United States Lines*)

Off and away on her sea trials in the spring of 1952. (*ALF Collection*)

The *United States* as seen from the decks of the departing *America*. (*ALF Collection*)

10

Tense Voyage:
Anna D'Ambrosio

On October 7, 1985, the 23,600-grt Italian cruise ship *Achille Lauro* made headlines around the world. A well-known ship in European circles, she was now known everywhere. In a brazen, lawless act, she was hijacked by Palestinian terrorists during one of her otherwise regular two-week cruises out of Genoa to ports in the eastern Mediterranean. She was held "captive" for three days. The world watched and waited as several nations had their military forces on alert and their ministers offering intervention.

"It was very tense, very frightening actually," recalled Anna D'Ambrosio, who was the ship's assistant purser at the time. Owned by Naples-based Lauro Lines, the 631-foot-long *Achille Lauro* had arrived in Alexandria, Egypt, in the early morning and quickly disembarked all but eighty-five of her 900 passengers for the all-day, overland tours down to Cairo. The ship then sailed to Port Said, where later that night the tour passengers would rejoin the ship.

"It was lunchtime, after leaving Alexandria harbor, that two terrorist-passengers went to the bridge and two others to the engine room," recalled Mrs D'Ambrosio, a native of Sorrento whom we met aboard another Italian-owned liner, the *Monterey*, in 1996 where she was hotel manager. "The terrorists had bazooka guns," she added. "They told the captain [Antonio Da Rosa] to put all crew members and passengers in the restaurant and to announce that the ship was now in Palestinian hands. Anyone refusing to obey would be shot!"

The terrorists cut all radio room communication and insisted that they had placed bombs throughout the ship. "There weren't any bombs, of course," added D'Ambrosio. "They also said that there were other terrorists among the remaining eighty-five passengers.

Two or three cruises previously, one of the terrorists had actually sailed on the *Achille Lauro* to study the ship."

The hijackers had the 22-knot liner go to Tartus in Syria, where they hoped to exchange political prisoners. "We went and then waited and waited," she recalled. "The passengers and crew slept on the lounge floor for three days. They could only use the toilets under guard. Finally, Yasser Arafat intervened and settled the situation. The *Achille Lauro* returned to Port Said, the terrorists surrendered, and then the ship sailed empty back to Genoa."

D'Ambrosio concluded, "Hundreds and hundreds of journalists, photographers, and television crews were on the pierside at Genoa. It was exciting, overwhelming, but also very tearful."

The entire affair had shattering, diverse effects on the cruise industry. There were rumors that the *Achille Lauro* would be renamed immediately, even sold. Running in a joint Lauro-Chandris Cruises service at the time, the Greek partner soon pulled out. A weakened economy in 1985–86 coupled with terrorist problems in Lebanon, Libya, and even at Athens airport, meant that Mediterranean cruising not only dropped, but crashed. One Greek cruise ship set off months later, in May 1986, with a scant six passengers aboard. Other cruise ships were laid up and even whole companies, such as Greece's K Lines, collapsed. It took time for the tarnish of the *Achille Lauro* affair to fade. The ship itself, built back in 1939–47 as Holland's *Willem Ruys*, sailed on for another nine years. But she had further misfortune. In December 1994, she caught fire and then sank off the Somalian coast while on an extended cruise from Genoa to Cape Town via the Suez.

The 1,500-passenger *Achille Lauro* arriving at Melbourne in February 1972. (*Frank Andrews Collection*)

Another view at Melbourne of the arriving *Achille Lauro*. (*Frank Andrews Collection*)

Having been commissioned in 1947 as the Dutch *Willem Ruys*, the *Achille Lauro* was rebuilt in 1964–65 and given a very modern look. (*Mick Lindsay Collection*)

Left: Outbound from Genoa on a two-week cruise to the Eastern Mediterranean. (*Author's Collection*)

Below: Visiting Sydney in 1992. (*Bill Barber Collection*)

11
British Merchant Service: John Malone

Running away to sea! In 1957, when John Malone was fifteen, he was just old enough to runaway to sea—as a galley boy aboard the once large Blue Star Line. He was off aboard one of the company's big freighters, the *Australia Star*, and his very first trip was a roaring introduction to life at sea—it was a trip around the world that took six months.

Sixty years later, John recalled, "We sailed from London down to South America, to Rio de Janeiro and Buenos Aires, then over to South Africa, to Cape Town, Port Elizabeth, and Durban. Then it was up to Lourenco Marques and Beira before heading across the Indian Ocean to New Zealand, to Wellington, Gisburn, Napier, and Auckland. We loaded meat in those ports. Then it was up to the Panama Canal, Kingston, Trinidad, Barbados, and finally home to London. It was quite an initiation— and I gained lots of experience. And it was an initiation to life itself. I earned 3 pounds or about $15 a week. When the other very young lads in the crew went ashore, we'd buy one drink each and then sip it for hours. We never had money for a taxi when returning to the ship."

John remained on British freighters for several years, sailing with the likes of the Royal Mail Lines, Harrison Line, Ellerman, Pacific Steam Navigation, and Houlder Brothers. "I did three trips on the Argentine meat run aboard the *Tewksbury* [Houlder Brothers] and remember seeing the cows being marched into the factory at one end and coming out in tin cans on the other! Going ashore, we'd sometimes go to dimly lit, little theaters and watch films on a small screen.

Seeing a movie cost about 20 cents in Argentina in the late '50s."

In 1960, John began a stint on passenger liners after joining Canadian Pacific and was assigned to the 25,000-ton *Empress of England*. "We made seventeen-day roundtrips between Liverpool, Quebec, and Montreal and then back to Liverpool," he recalled. "We had the three liners and each had a different personality. Each ship even worked differently. But the *Empress of Canada* was then brand new [1961], the flagship and, in ways, the most stringent."

"We had great fun on the Empress liners," Malone. "We would have three-night layovers at Montreal and five at Liverpool during these crossings. We would leave Liverpool's Prince's Landing Stage on Tuesdays, having arrived on the previous Thursdays. On the other end, we would arrive in Montreal on Monday mornings and sail on Wednesday afternoons. We carried lots and lots of immigrants, mostly from England and Scotland, on the westbound sailings. Quebec City was the primary port of entry. Canadian Pacific worked closely with the Canadian Government on this. The liners were still the cheaper way to cross the Atlantic in the early '60s. Cargo, especially mail, was an important consideration on these crossings as well."

Later assigned to the *Empress of Canada*, John concluded, "The crew made money in all sorts of ways. Some of the galley boys sold passenger food to crewmembers. Some earned large tips. Some shared their work and then shared their tips. And some just gambled and were lucky—sometimes very lucky."

With her very prominent funnel, the freighter *Auckland Star* offloads in the London Docks. (*Mick Lindsay Collection*)

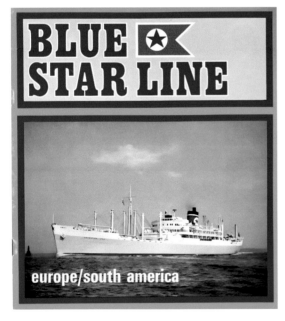

Above left: Blue Star Line ran a quartet of fifty-passenger ships been London and the East Coast of South America. (*Author's Collection*)

Above right: In the final heyday of British passenger shipping, Blue Star maintained offices at Lower Regent Street in London. (*Author's Collection*)

Seen at Liverpool: The *Empress of Canada* is on the right, with the *Kungsholm* behind, visiting on a Western Europe–British Isles cruise. (*Author's Collection*)

The 650-foot-long *Empress of Canada* went on to become the *Mardi Gras*, the first ship (in 1972) for Carnival Cruise Lines. (*Author's Collection*)

Above: Crossing between Liverpool and Montreal on Canadian Pacific. (*Author's Collection*)

Left: Evocative advertising for the final three Empress liners. (*Author's Collection*)

Above: The *Empress of England* outbound from New York and in an ice-filled Hudson River. (*Moran Towing & Transportation Co.*)

Right: Six-day fares across the Atlantic began at $175 in the early 1960s. (*Norman Knebel Collection*)

12
Umbrellas in the Lounge: Giuseppe Cocurullo

When Mediterranean Shipping Company's *Achille Lauro* burned and then sank off East Africa early in December 1994, it was a great loss. Among other problems, that 23,600-ton ship was bound for a long and valuable cruising charter in South Africa. But now there was a gap, a big gap. Fortunately, MSC Cruises—as the ship's Italian-Swiss owners are called—had just bought Costa Cruises' 13,600-ton *Enrico Costa*. But she was still at Genoa, awaiting an extensive refit before becoming MSC's *Symphony* and then later making her debut in Mediterranean, cruising out of Genoa. Suddenly, that ship was needed in South African waters, at Durban, to assume the charter intended for the ill-fated *Achille Lauro*.

"I was at home in Sorrento [near Naples] and sick in bed with the flu when I saw the *Achille Lauro* burn and sink on Italian television," remembered Captain Giuseppe Cocurullo. "I was still quite ill when, two or three days later, MSC's Naples office called to say that I must join the *Enrico Costa/Symphony* at Genoa. She had not yet completed her refit, but needed to leave Genoa in three days for Durban."

The 580-foot-long *Symphony* was forty-four years old at the time. The 18-knot ship had been built just after the war in 1950 for French owners (Marseilles-based Transport Maritimes) but at a British shipyard, Swan, Hunter & Wigham Richardson at Newcastle. Then named *Provence*, she sailed on the Marseilles–East Coast of South America run, carrying up to 1,284 passengers in four classes. In 1963, she did some charter cruising out of New York for the otherwise short-lived Caribbean Cruise Lines. She made weekly, seven-night trips to Bermuda and Nassau with minimum fares of $195.

The twin-screw ship was sold to Costa in 1965, becoming the *Enrico C* and then, in 1983, changing to *Enrico Costa*. Early on, she continued on the South American run for Costa, but later ran only cruises: the Mediterranean, Northern Europe, and, in winter, in South America. She was extensively refitted in 1989. Finally outmoded when Costa expanded their fleet with bigger, newer ships, she was sold to Mediterranean Shipping in September 1994.

"Unfortunately, we had a big task in front of us," said Captain Cocurullo as he remembered his first visit to the ship at Genoa in December 1994. "She was in very poor condition. The Italian authorities did not even want to renew her operating certificate because of the deterioration. But we finally left Genoa—and in three days. A hundred crew were aboard. We reached Durban on Christmas Eve. During the fifteen-day voyage to South Africa, we cleaned and painted day and night. But there was leakage and flooding everywhere. Pipes were cracked and bursting. We had to work in the lounges with umbrellas! 200 more crew met us in Durban. They were South Africans and Madagascans. For most of them, it was their very first time at sea. Fortunately, we succeeded—our very first cruise was a happy one. Travelers had been suspicious following the fire aboard *Achille Lauro*, but soon they found the *Symphony* to be a pleasant, well-run ship. Soon word spread—and we were fully booked. Later, the ship was based fulltime in South African waters. MSC Cruises from Durban became well known as a great experience, a wonderful adventure!"

Above: The *Enrico C* seen at Genoa. (*Author's Collection*)

Right: Costa cruising in 1961. (*Norman Knebel Collection*)

13

Off to Sea:
John Jones

Off to sea! John Jones was a mere boy of fifteen when he walked into the huge and very grand Cunard building in his native Liverpool. "A man that seemed to be 10-feet tall took me to a room, placed me against a wall, and measured my height. Happily, I was just tall enough," recalled John. "I was soon off to training school and then assigned to the *Scythia*, then thirty years old and sailing on the Liverpool to Quebec City run. I earned £7 a month or 5p an hour. I was given a crimson uniform and pillbox hat—and off I went. After that, I had to buy my own uniforms from a London tailor on Saville Row. I was a Cunard bellboy. We were said to be the youngest seamen in the British merchant navy and, as a group, we slept ten to twelve to a room. We ran errands on board, delivered telegrams and other messages, helped in the purser's office, and sometimes sat and chatted with passengers, especially ladies in first class, who were traveling alone. One grand lady once had four bellboys sitting at her feet!"

John was soon posted to another veteran Cunarder, the *Franconia*. "She went aground in the St Lawrence, near Quebec City [July 1950], and then needed weeks of repairs. Many of the crew took jobs in the nearby Chateau Frontenac Hotel to stay busy, but mostly to earn extra money."

Afterward, John became what he called a "gypsy." He served with Canadian Pacific, aboard the *Empress of Canada* and *Empress of France*, with Pacific Steam Navigation and their *Reina Del Pacifico* and *Reina Del Mar*, on the troopship *Empire Clyde*, and on the migrant ship *Georgic*. "While with Cunard, I was something of one of those 'Cunard Yanks,' bringing home clothes, food, and records from New York. We'd all go to Macy's and Woolworths. We also went to the Market Diner on 12th Avenue and 52nd Street, where the third drink was always free for seamen."

John also recalled, "On the West Coast of South America run, we had lots of colonial-type passengers plus lots of businessmen on the *Reina Del Pacifico* and *Reina Del Mar* It was still three-class and I recall that first class was really too quiet, even too dull, and so these rich, well-dressed passengers would often march down to more casual, fun-filled tourist class in the evenings. Aboard the *Empire Clyde*, we carried troops, guns, and military equipment for the planned British invasion of Egypt in 1956. As for the *Georgic*, which still had damage from being bombed and set afire in the war, she was said to be the 'roughest' passenger ship in the entire British fleet. She was really not fit for regular passenger service. Regular Cunard crews did not want to sail aboard her and sometimes there were too few crew. It was said that Cunard would go to prisons in and around Liverpool and gather-up minor criminals to serve on board. These crew members were known to cause problems such as brawls and create problems with the police in ports of call. They once called a sudden strike in Cape Town and would not re-board the ship, and another time the ship itself was actually banned from Australian ports. When I served aboard the *Georgic*, we carried 10-pound Poms, those British migrants out to Sydney. Then we sailed up to Malaya, carrying Australian troops. Then it was to Vietnam and a charter to the French. We carried troops and evacuees out of troubled French Indochina. The troops were a rough lot that included wounded, diseased and some hired Africans. We delivered them on a long, hot voyage to Algiers and then to Marseilles."

John was also posted to another Cunarder, the freighter *Alsatia*, which was on the London–New York run. "We went, in the dark of a late night, to the rescue of the sinking American freighter *Flying Enterprise*. She was foundering off the British coast, off Cornwall. We were ready with blankets, medicines, and lots of hot soup."

John was soon back to passenger ships by the mid-1950s, however. He continued to be that "gypsy" and sailed aboard Shaw Savill Line, Union-Castle, New Zealand Shipping Company, and the exotic Booth Line. At Shaw Savill, he sailed in two of the company's oldest if smaller liners. "The *Mataroa* & *Tamaroa*, used on the long New Zealand run, were two of the oldest and slowest passenger ships in the British fleet by then," he recalled. "It took six weeks to go from London to Auckland via Curacao and the Panama Canal. Occasionally, we'd stop at Pitcairn Island to land supplies and mail. The locals, who were expert rowers, would come out to the anchored ship in open boats. They were very spiritual people. Once, these open boats were caught in a fierce, tropical storm. But they all continued to row as they sang hymns. After arriving in New Zealand, we'd stay in local ports for six weeks, mostly loading lamb to be brought back to England. I made extra money by working as a temporary docker. But once I missed the ship and was taken to jail as a deserter. The jail for two nights was awful—a straw mattress for a bed and meager rations for food. After I was freed, I was flown—under police guard—to the South Island to rejoin the *Mataroa*. I was taken aboard, brought before the captain, and fined a week's pay plus the cost for the jail, police, and plane ride. I returned to London with no money—not a penny!"

The veteran Cunarder *Scythia* loading vintage automobiles at Liverpool. (*Cunard Line*)

Dating from 1921, the *Scythia* is seen here at New York's Pier 92 in a view dated 1955. (*Author's Collection*)

The *Reina Del Mar* in the River Mersey at Liverpool. (*Author's Collection*)

The veteran Shaw Savill Line passenger ship *Mataroa*. (*Author's Collection*)

The migrant ship *Georgic* arriving in Australia with some 1,900 migrants on board. (*ALF Collection*)

The all-tourist-class *Bloemfontein Castle* was purposely intended for the migrant trade to South and East Africa. (*Author's Collection*)

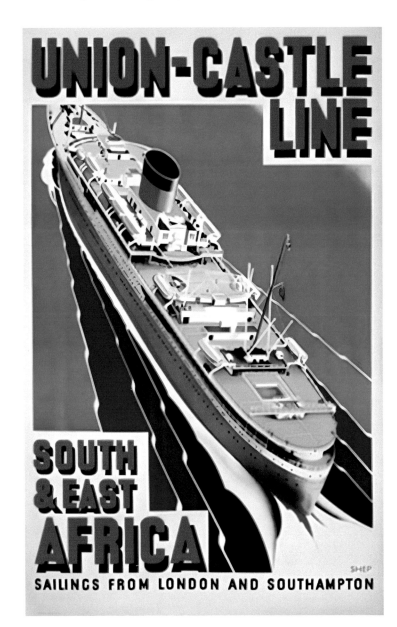

Left: Union-Castle Line was a standard setter of services to and from Africa. (*Norman Knebel Collection*)

Below: The classic passenger-cargo liner *Rangitane* passing Gravesend after departing London. (*Mick Lindsay Collection*)

Right: The *Rangitoto* on a rare visit to Melbourne. (*Tim Noble Collection*)

Below: New Zealand Shipping Company was also known as the New Zealand Line. (*Norman Knebel Collection*)

The combination passenger-cargo liner *Hubert* seen anchored in the Amazon River. (*Mick Lindsay Collection*)

Home from West Africa, Elder Dempster Lines' *Apapa* offloads at Liverpool. (*Mick Lindsay Collection*)

John also served aboard Union-Castle's *Bloemfontein Castle*, an all-tourist-class ship designed purposely for immigrants and low-fare travelers. "We carried lots of British migrants going out to Rhodesia, but also stopped in Rotterdam and collected Dutch and German migrants as well. Often, they were very poor people. When we'd reach Africa, on their last day on board, they'd steal food from the dining room. They had no money for food for even their first days ashore."

With the London-based New Zealand Shipping Company, John served on the 21,000-ton *Rangitoto*, which carried over 400 passengers in all one-class quarters. "NZ Shipping, as it was called, was said to be a cut above Shaw Savill," he remembered. "Their ships were faster and more comfortable."

The Booth Line, also British, maintained an unusual service—across the mid-Atlantic from Liverpool to the Caribbean and then 1,000 miles up to the Amazon River to Manaus. He sailed aboard that company's passenger ships: the *Hilary*, *Hildebrand*, and *Hubert*. "These voyages along the Amazon were hot, steamy, thickly humid. The crew would often sleep on deck. Below, if you opened a porthole, insects of all sizes and types would come flooding in! The ships' navigating officers had to be very careful because of submerged rocks and floating logs in the river.

Once, we bent the ship's only screw and then limped to Manaus. There was no shipyard in such a remote place and so two Brazilian divers were hired to make repairs. They carved away some of the twisted steel, which actually made the ship faster than before. The chief engineer was more than surprised—and pleased! We carried businessmen, traders, and sometimes even a few tourists in first class, and missionaries, medical people, and teachers in tourist class. The crew often bought parrots and birds in Manaus and then brought them home to Liverpool. Myself, I bought a little Cayman, kept it in my cabin, but then discovered it didn't like colder climates. Soon after landing in Liverpool, I gave it to the Chester Zoo. Liverpool customs were easy in those days. Give them a few pounds and almost anything could be brought in!"

By the early 1960s, John was to go to another passenger ship, the *Apapa* of Elder Dempster Lines, serving on the Liverpool–West Africa run, but he was hired—almost at the last minute—by Lockheed Aircraft's Liverpool plant. "I was sent for training and became a skilled craftsman—making precision aircraft parts. My life as a seaman—of working ten hours a day and seventy hours a week—was wonderful, a great education in itself, but it was then over."

14

On the Run to Bermuda: Ron Evans

Ron Evans worked for several British passenger ships in the early 1950s. "It was a great life for those times. Britain was still caught up in austerity and rationing, and by traveling overseas we could buy food and bring it home," he recalled. "I'd worked on P&O liners, but my favorite was the Furness-Bermuda Line. My favorite ship was the *Ocean Monarch*, which was like a big yacht and carried only little more than 400 passengers. Mostly, she was on the forty-hour run between New York and Bermuda. Charlie Chuckles was the captain of the ship, and it was said he knew every sandbank around Bermuda.

The ship made mostly six-day cruises and was often filled with single American women. We'd have an overnight on Fridays at Pier 95 in New York and the Market Diner was the place where all the guys used to meet. In those days, we were always dressed when we went ashore—always in suits and ties."

"Later, I served on the *Queen of Bermuda*, also on the six-day run out of New York," he concluded. "Working on those Furness ships, I was considered a 'first class waiter' and later I found work ashore—in the best hotels in New York City and Miami Beach."

Three o'clock on a Saturday afternoon and the grand *Queen of Bermuda* sails from Pier 95, New York. (*Author's Collection*)

The yacht-like *Ocean Monarch* at Bermuda. (*ALF Collection*)

Starlit Nights...luxury cruising by Furness

Left: "Starlit nights" on a six-day cruise aboard the *Ocean Monarch*. (*Norman Knebel Collection*)

Below: Fond farewell: The last sailing of the *Ocean Monarch* from New York in August 1966. (*ALF Collection*)

The 516-foot-long *Ocean Monarch* moored at Front Street in Hamilton, Bermuda. (*ALF Collection*)

The *Queen of Bermuda* could carry up to 730 passengers. (*ALF Collection*)

Above: A new look: The *Queen of Bermuda* was rebuilt and modernized with a single funnel in 1961–62. (*Author's Collection*)

Right: Furness-Bermuda Line advertising dated 1960. (*Author's Collection*)

BERMUDA

Furness "LiV-ABOARD" Cruises

The smartest shops and restaurants are just across the street when you live on board your Furness Cruise ship. Entertainment, air conditioned dining, dancing, deck sports, swimming pool. Three delicious meals daily. One Luxury Class only, every cabin with private bath, 6 days . . . $153 up.

BERMUDA-NASSAU CRUISES Sept. 29 — 8 days $200 up Dec. 23 — 10 days $250 up	**ALSO** Summer Cruises to the breeze-cool West Indies and Canada's romantic Saguenay.
REGULAR BERMUDA SERVICE $125 up roundtrip from New York	**THRIFT SEASON** rates in Dec. and Jan., 6-day "Liv-Aboard" Bermuda Cruises $125 up.

SS QUEEN OF BERMUDA · SS OCEAN MONARCH

See Your TRAVEL AGENT or

FURNESS BERMUDA LINE

Opposite above: Aside from the *Queen Mary*, the *Queen of Bermuda* was the last three-funnel liner to sail from New York. (*ALF Collection*)

Opposite below: The *Queen of Bermuda* at Pier 95, New York. (*ALF Collection*)

15

Cruise Director: Rick Spath

A morning TV show, staff meetings, a walk around the decks, introducing guest speakers, and then, by evening, it is showtime and more introductions. The life of a cruise director is indeed not just a busy one, but a very busy one. And one of the very best on all the seas is Rick Spath, a shipboard friend of some twenty-five years by 2007. We were together aboard the *Crystal Serenity*, crossing the mid-Atlantic from Miami to Lisbon with a day in Bermuda *en route*. With an entertainment department staff of 100 under his watchful eye, Rick provided a grand program of amusements and diversions. The voyage also had a theme: big band music.

Rick and I were both born in Hoboken, that New Jersey community that was the setting for Hollywood's *On the Waterfront*. We were both drawn to education, becoming teachers. I stayed, working with sixth graders for thirty-two years; Rick had a much shorter stint before being drawn to life aboard the liners, almost inhaling the smell of the salt air.

"It all started back in 1979 when I was hired to help put up Christmas decorations on board the *QE2*," he recalled. "She was a very different ship in those days, more formal mostly. I sailed from New York to Fort Lauderdale, then got off while the ship cruised the Caribbean for the holidays. I rejoined at Fort Lauderdale and sailed back to New York, taking down all the decorations. I was so impressed with the white-suited cruise director. I started with Scott Peterson, who today is also a Crystal cruise director and subsequent hotel director. The cruise director on the *QE2* later suggested that I myself become a cruise director. Eventually, I was hired by Cunard and joined the sisters *Cunard Countess* and *Cunard Princess*."

But Rick soon moved on, like a port of call, to the legendary Home Lines. "I fell hopelessly in love with the *Oceanic*, my very favorite ship only after the *Rotterdam* [of 1959]. I also sailed on the *Doric* and the *Atlantic*, both also with Home Lines. My best years ever were on the Home Lines. I never, ever wanted to take a vacation! It was like being part of one, big family, with both the crew and the guests.

It was also classic cruising. There were even great bon voyage parties at New York. We have, say, 1,000 passengers sailing with 2–3,000 visitors."

While on vacation from Home Lines, Rick went off and moonlighted on another company with an Italian tone and style. "I served on two great ships, the *Fairsea* and the *Fairwind*, of Sitmar Cruises," he added. "Sitmar was another fantastic company. They had great quality of service and the most attentive sense of detail. They were absolutely right when they called it 'the Sitmar Experience'. Working for the likes of Home Lines and Sitmar Cruises was the best foundation for me. Both companies were great training grounds."

Next stop on Rick's cruising evolution was the great Holland America Line. "I'd had a very quick stay at Bahama Star Line and sailed aboard their little *Vera Cruz*, but then joined HAL. I joined them in 1984, just as the sisters *Nieuw Amsterdam* and *Noordam* were commissioned, and stayed fifteen years, until 1998. They too are a great company, offering a wonderful experience. I did the *Rotterdam* world cruises, which were so lavish, and the Big Band Cruises, which included the likes of the exceptional Rosemary Clooney."

Then it was to brand-new Disney Cruise Lines in '98. "They did not have an actual cruise director, but a cruise director that was more like a hotel director. Disney wanted a theme park at sea at the time. They were a very unusual company to work for and were very much 'handcuffed' to their ways. They had two beautiful new ships, the *Disney Magic* and *Disney Wonder*."

Rick's diverse experiences next took him to Celebrity, where he served on the *Infinity* for a short time, but then it was time to join Crystal. With his expert skills, great charm, and high, seemingly endless energy, he has been serving aboard the 1,060-passenger *Crystal Serenity* ever since. Indeed, Crystal is very fortunate to have the services of the great Rick Spath. Assuredly, he is one of the very best cruise directors in the industry!

Above: Home Lines' *Atlantic* departing from New York on a Saturday afternoon. (*Author's Collection*)

Right: Sun-Way Cruises on the very popular Home Lines. (*Author's Collection*)

The luxurious *Crystal Symphony* at Port Everglades. (*Port of Port Everglades Authority*)

The 748-foot-long *Rotterdam* was the new flagship of Holland America Line beginning in 1959. (*Author's Collection*)

Above left: Between seven-day cruises to Alaska, the *Rotterdam* pauses at Vancouver. (*ALF Collection*)

Above right: The 1,456-passenger *Rotterdam* on her maiden call at Southampton in September 1959. (*Author's Collection*)

Below: The very popular *Oceanic* departs from New York. (*Author's Collection*)

The 774-foot-long *Oceanic* was one of the most beautiful and important liners of the 1960s. (*Home Lines*)

The *Rotterdam* departing for a seven-night cruise to Bermuda and Nassau. (*Author's Collection*)

16
Blue Funnel to Eastern Waters: Alan Gilchrist

The Blue Funnel Line was, until the 1980s, one of Britain's greatest shipowners. Liverpool based, they had over fifty ships, almost all freighters, all of them with names from Greek mythology like *Jason*, *Hector*, *Pyrrhus*, *Prometheus*, and *Ixion* and, rather expectedly, all with distinctive blue-painted funnels (with black tops). Blue Funnel was then hugely successful, busily plying the freighter trades between the U.K. and North European ports out East—via the Mediterranean and the Suez Canal to Far Eastern ports such as Singapore, Penang, Manila, Hong Kong, Kobe, and Yokohama. A secondary trade went to Australian ports: Fremantle, Brisbane, Hobart, Melbourne, and Sydney.

"In the then-huge British Merchant Navy [with over 5,000 ships and 55,000 related staff in 1960], Blue Funnel was considered a wonderful company to sail with. Myself, I felt they were just superb. You could trust them. Around Liverpool in those days, Harrison Line, also British, was said to be among the worst. Harrison was rather notorious for poor conditions and the worst food," recalled Alan Gilchrist, a ship's engineer. We met on a recent Cunard voyage, aboard the *Queen Elizabeth*. "Blue Funnel's headquarters were in the India Buildings in Liverpool. They had some great ships, all very sturdy and sound, well maintained and well run. Along with five or six holds of freight, many of them carried up to twelve passengers—in six double-bedded cabins.

Eight of them, however, had space for thirty passengers, which meant they carried a doctor. They were very popular ships, in fact, with people who wanted or could afford a long, leisurely voyage. It took five weeks to go from Liverpool to Hong Kong, for example. On the freighters, a full voyage might take four or five months. Once, as I remember, the *Ascanius* was gone from Liverpool for ten months."

"All passengers boarded or left at Liverpool," added Alan. "The sea staff was paid-off and separate 'shore officers and crew' arrived. Known as the 'shore gangs,' they would take the ships—for cargo purposes only—for about two weeks to U.K. and European ports such as Glasgow, Newcastle, London, Hamburg, Rotterdam, and Antwerp. Blue Funnel was the only company, as far as I remember, that had two crews for each ship—the sea staff and these 'shore gangs.' Blue Funnel was also noted to have some of the best engineers in the British Merchant Navy. They knew their stuff!

"They were kept busy—many of the company's ships had Harland & Wolff engines, which were notably very difficult and very heavy to work. Other ships in the fleet had Danish-made B&W diesels, which were also difficult. Blue Funnel [now long gone from shipping] was a wonderful company. They were part of a great era."

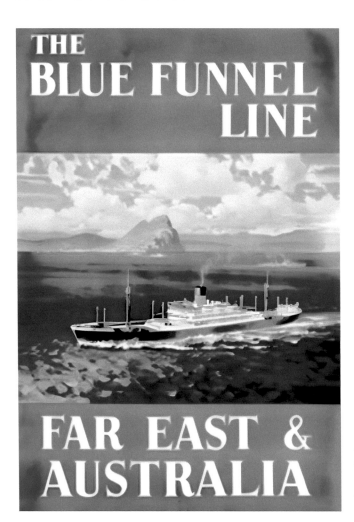

Left: Blue Funnel Line was a well-known British shipping company. (*Norman Knebel Collection*)

Below: The thirty-passenger *Jason* arriving off Sydney. (*Author's Collection*)

17
On the Run to West Africa: Tony Costello

Liverpool-born Tony Costello was in the "seamen's pool" of the still huge British Merchant Navy in the 1960s. The pool meant that he rotated between ships and shipping lines. One of his assignments was the passenger ship *Accra*, a smallish passenger ship which belonged to the Elder Dempster Lines, a British firm that traded to West Africa. "We sailed from Liverpool as far as Lagos. The ship carried about 300 passengers in two classes. We had government and business passengers mostly, and occasionally the odd tourist. But once when we were sailing between the West African ports (Takoradi, Lagos, and Freetown), we also carried as many as 400 deck passengers, all of them Africans who were housed under canvas tents on the forward cargo decks. They were mostly migrant workers, usually heading between Takoradi and Freetown in Sierra Leone—and they traveled with everything, including the kitchen sink! They even brought goats and chickens along. The voyage usually took four days. Elder Dempster erected special toilets for them in the fo'c'sle and there were washing facilities in the tween decks. They did not mix with the regular passengers."

"Whole tribes would travel on ships like the *Accra*," recalled Costello. "They would arrive aboard and leave the ship in a metal bucket that had about six seats. It would be lifted or lowered over the side as the *Accra* was in midstream, at anchor. The chiefs would often sail as well and would get the best place over the hatch and under the canvas tent. Everyone, it seemed, would wait on him and attend to him."

Costello concluded, "In the '60s, West African ports were said to be the most congested and crowded in the world. Passenger ships had priority and were given berths, but for freighters, special payoffs had to be made to port officials to get a berth. Many freighters simply anchored in midstream and huge logs were floated downriver and moored on both sides of the ship. These logs were loaded aboard and carried back to the U.K. At Elder Dempster, we always got out of ports as fast as we could. There were endless delays. Some ships sometimes waited at anchor for as long as nine or ten montahs!"

The *Accra* of Elder Dempster was a classic smaller passenger-cargo ship built just after World War II. (*Author's Collection*)

The yacht-like *Aureol* was the flagship of Elder Dempster Lines. (*S. W. Rawlings*)

18
British Banana Boats:
Alan Hulse

Elders & Fyffes Limited, also known as the Fyffes Line, was noted for their smart-looking, all-white "banana boats." Still trading today, but now using chartered tonnage, the earlier British flagships of Fyffes had an added romance about them—they sailed to the exotic islands of the Caribbean. They carried U.K.-made manufactured goods outbound and, expectedly, returned often with large loads of bananas—sometimes over 100,000 bunches. By the '60s, their freighters carried up to the customary twelve passengers; their two passenger-cargo liners, the *Golfito* and *Camito*, had accommodations for as many as 100.

In the '60s, Alan Hulse sailed as crew with Fyffes. "I sailed aboard the Fyffes freighters, some of which were quite fast. We'd cross over to Barbados, Trinidad, Grenada, and then to Jamaica, to Kingston and Port Antonio. Homeward, we'd land at Southampton or sometimes at Avonmouth. The port was selected by which one had the best rates for offloading the bananas. Our

big competitor in those days was another British company, the Geest Line."

"Fyffes was a very nice company to work for," added Hulse. "Myself, I was a young seaman struck with wanderlust. Coming from Liverpool, I wanted to see new places. The routes on Fyffes seemed exotic—palm trees, sandy beaches, lots of sun. We often carried up to twelve passengers, mostly older, retired types in winter, who took the entire six-week roundtrips. They escaped at least part of the cold, dreary winters in England. But once, I remember, we had only two passengers aboard, a honeymoon couple. They had the ship to themselves, but we rarely saw them. Afterward, my next stop was to see South America so I joined another British shipping line, Pacific Steam Navigation Company, which sailed from the U.K. to the Caribbean as well, but then passed through the Panama Canal and touched on ports all along the West Coast of South America as far south as Valparaiso."

The 100-passenger *Golfito* departing from Southampton. (*Mick Lindsay Collection*)

19
Union-Castle to Cape Town: Trevor Blackwell

ike many young men following World War II, Trevor Blackwell joined the Merchant Navy. He shipped out from Southampton beginning in the late 1940s on such well-known liners as the *Athlone Castle*, *Warwick Castle*, and *Carnarvon Castle.* "They sailed on the mail run [in 1950–51], two weeks in each direction, to Cape Town, Port Elizabeth, East London and Durban," he recalled. "We were young fellows, six to ten to a cabin. There was never a dull moment and lots of fun, even if we worked eleven hours a day, seven days a week. The 'glory hole' steward used to come around at 6 in the morning as a wake-up call. Then it was scrub out, take a shower, get changed, and then go to serve two sittings of breakfast. Between, we cleaned the lino floors and polished the silver. Everything had to be immaculate. Then it was lunch followed by afternoon tea. Dinner started at 6, again for two sittings, and then, before bed, a stop in the Pig & Whistle. You could buy a beer in those days for 10 cents."

South to the Sun on Union-Castle Line. (*Norman Knebel Collection*)

Above: One of the older liners on the Express Mail Service between Southampton and South Africa was the *Winchester Castle*, built in 1930. (*Author's Collection*)

Right: Well known in 1950s and '60s travel circles, there was a sailing every Thursday afternoon from Southampton. (*Norman Knebel Collection*)

Left: Loading at Southampton before heading south. (*Author's Collection*)

Below: The *Pretoria Castle*, seen at Southampton, could carry up to 755 passengers—214 in first class and 541 in tourist class. (*Author's Collection*)

Right: A large, foldout passenger accommodation plan for the *Edinburgh Castle.*
(*Author's Collection*)

Below: Numerous passenger ships were idle during the big British maritime strike
in May–June 1966. Alone, this view shows ten idle passenger ships at Southampton.
(*Author's Collection*)

The *Rhodesia Castle*, which was based in London, was used on Union-Castle's alternate passenger service around the African continent. (*Union-Castle Line*)

Another view of idle ships during the devastating strike of 1966. From left to right: *Good Hope Castle*, *Reina Del Mar*, and *Edinburgh Castle*. (*Author's Collection*)

20
On Board P&O's *Chusan*:
Robert Leslie

obert Leslie recalled, "My favorite P&O liner in the 1950s was the *Chusan*. She was not used on the well-known service to Australia, but was assigned to the P&O's Far East service—London–Suez–Bombay–Singapore–Hong Kong–Japan run. Altogether, it took four months to make a roundtrip. The *Chusan*, at 24,000 tons and carrying up to 1,000 passengers, was slightly smaller than, say, the *Himalaya*, *Arcadia*, and *Iberia*. But the *Chusan* had something special—a warmth and altogether a nice, friendly feeling about her. She might have looked like the others, but she was different—and many P&O passengers and crew felt the same. On the *Chusan*, we made P&O's very first world cruise, well world voyage. The year was 1958, as I remember. We sailed out to Hong Kong and then on to Kobe and Yokohama, but instead of reversing and heading home to London, we crossed the Pacific to Honolulu and then over to Los Angeles and San Francisco. We then sailed up to Vancouver and then went off on a two-week cruise to Hawaii, then returned to California and finally sailed home to London, stopping at Acapulco, the Panama Canal, and the Caribbean. On that leg, and for the first time aboard the *Chusan*, we had more American than British passengers on board. P&O wanted to develop, to cultivate, the American West Coast passenger & tourist market."

Above left: The very popular *Chusan* departing from Melbourne. (*Tim Noble Collection*)

Above right: Another view of the 672-foot-long *Chusan* at Melbourne. (*Tim Noble Collection*)

Above left: At sea on board the *Chusan* in a view dated 1969. (*Tim Noble Collection*)

Above right: A 1950s P&O poster. (*Author's Collection*)

Left: The *Chusan* berthed in Sydney. (*Bill Barber Collection*)

21
Fly Cruises to the Med: Brenton Jenkins

A longtime friend, Brenton Jenkins, had been Cunard's senior purser in the 1960s. But he later recalled his post-Cunard days, after 1968, aboard the old *Queen Frederica*. "I read recently in one of your books of the *Queen Frederica*. It brought back many memories for me. I worked for Captain Ted Langton, owner of Sovereign Cruises, headquartered at Maddox St in London, from 1967 to 1972, when he started up the first fly cruises from the U.K. to the Med. They were on the *Queen Frederica*, chartered from Anthony Chandris. It was my job to develop a completely new system of organization on board the vessel, finding all the British staff to operate the hotel side, whereas the deck and engine remained Greek from Chandris Lines itself. I was then sailing on all the cruises as the onboard Charter's Representative and running the hotel side. Altogether, I loved every moment—and the Greeks kept that great old ship beautifully running. They were wonderful years for me after the 'glory days' of Cunard. My mother was often on board. Captain Langton was very kind—she could join me anytime and always gave her a suite.

"My mother traveled with her friend Maude Brown, who could also come for free. Then there was Elizabeth Sayers from Cunard running the purser's office for me.

"The cruise staff included the young David de Havilland, the entertainment officer. He started his seagoing career with me after coming from the British Holiday Camp on Hayling Island. It was a long time ago, but so many good memories."

Above left: The *Queen Frederica* at Southampton, while under charter to Sovereign Cruises. (*Mick Lindsay Collection*)

Above right: Repairs: The 582-foot-long *Queen Frederica* in dry dock at Southampton. (*Mick Lindsay Collection*)

22
Aboard the Luxurious *Caronia*: Tony Bannon

Well over fifty years ago, in 1962, Liverpool-born Tony Bannon was young, adventurous, and decided the best thing was to go to sea. He sailed on a few freighters at first, but then being in the "seamen's pool," he was assigned to the famed Cunard Line as an AB, an able-bodied seaman. He was very fortunate. While undergoing its annual refit in the big Gladstone Dock at Liverpool, he was assigned to what some said was Cunard's most luxurious liner, the all-green *Caronia*.

"The *Caronia* was in dry dock for fifteen days and I stood watch," he remembered. "In those days, the *Caronia* was legendary—legendary for luxury, for carrying mostly very rich Americans, and for being one of the very best ships to join in the entire British Merchant Navy. I signed-on—this most luxurious of liners. After the New Year, in 1963, we were off on a three-week cruise from Southampton to the sun—to Barbados, Trinidad, Kingston, Nassau, and Bermuda—carrying lots of British passengers going to hotels and resorts and perhaps their homes in the Caribbean. Afterward, we sailed to New York—with only as few as 100 passengers—to begin the ship's program of long, luxurious cruises.

We did 100 days around the world and then eight weeks around the Mediterranean, which ended in Southampton. Next, we crossed to New York in June and did a forty-five-day North Cape cruise followed by another eight weeks around the Mediterranean.

"The *Caronia* was a beautiful ship and offered the best service in the entire Cunard fleet, even slightly better than first class on the bigger *Queen Mary* and *Queen Elizabeth*. The *Caronia* was also known as a 'happy ship.' The *Queens* had prestige according to Cunard crews, but the *Caronia* had luxury. Working on board was like winning the lottery. There was even a canvas pool for the crew on the foredeck. No one worked hard on the *Caronia*—there were 600 of Cunard's best staff to look after 300–400 passengers. There were crew that joined the ship from the maiden voyage in 1948 and stayed with her to the very last voyage in 1967. And as some crew grew older, they were deliberately kept on and given easier jobs. The crew also helped one another, often with finances if someone was caught short. It was often said that the *Caronia* [34,000 tons] was like a big yacht. I stayed with the *Caronia* for a year and loved every minute. And I saw much of the world in that year."

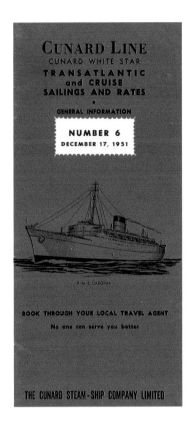

Above left: A Cunard sailing schedule for 1951. (*Author's Collection*)

Above right: The strikingly handsome *Caronia*. (*Cunard Line*)

Right: During a fall Mediterranean cruise, the *Caronia* is anchored off Villefranche. (*Cunard Line*)

23
Bibby to Burma: Robert Gordon

Robert Gordon sailed as a steward on Bibby Line combination passenger-cargo ships almost until the last voyages in the early '60s. There was the *Worcestershire*, *Staffordshire*, and, the last of them, the seventy-five-passenger *Leicestershire* and *Warwickshire*.

"We had government and business people mostly and sometimes with their entire families, but we also sold the long trips out to Rangoon and back as a sort of cruise," he recalled.

"Emphasis was placed on the relaxing, very healthy days at sea. Daily life for the passengers was quite simple. There were of course the three meals and afternoon tea. But after dinner, it might be just egg and spoon races or a quiz or just listening to records. It might seem boring, particularly by today's busy cruise liner standards, but we had passengers that preferred being bored—well, being very comfortably bored."

Carrying up to seventy-six passengers, the *Warwickshire* traded on Bibby Line's Burma service. (*Author's Collection*)

24
Tipping on Union-Castle: Geoff Edwards

Sailing on the great liners! "You made me realize [with your lectures] I was part of a golden, vanished age," noted Geoff Edwards, who sailed for five years as a cabin steward aboard Union-Castle Line's *Transvaal Castle*. "We were on the U.K.–South Africa mail run, the express service. We carried some very interesting passengers—and some very rich ones as well.

They were almost always well mannered, sometimes very kind and even friendly, but almost always very frugal—they rarely gave out decent tips. They felt that service, even very good and attentive service, was part of the fare. On this current trip [2015] aboard the *Queen Mary 2*, we are in the Princess Grill. We won't dream about not tipping!"

Above left: A 1957 sailing schedule for Union-Castle Line. (*Author's Collection*)

Above right: Flagship of the fleet: The imposing *Windsor Castle* departing from Cape Town. (*Union-Castle Line*)

Above left: It was dubbed "Royal Mail Service" to and from South Africa. (*Author's Collection*)

Above right: The *Windsor Castle* could carry up to 822 passengers in first- and tourist-class quarters. (*Author's Collection*)

25

Post-War Luxury: Jim Eldridge

Post-war luxury! Jim Eldridge came forward, aged and struggling with a cane, but friendly and positive. He attended my talks on the *Queen Elizabeth* (2016) and told me, "When I was sixteen, in 1948, I was hired by Cunard's main office, that big, imposing office block overlooking the Mersey at Liverpool, as a bellboy. I was lucky to have a job. It was just after the war and things in Britain were grim, dark, really quite depressing. But someone at Cunard must have liked me—I was sent to the brand-new *Caronia*, just completed and said to be the most luxurious big liner in the world. And she was—she was not just a floating hotel, but very much like a very grand floating club. Cunard's best—and possibly richest—passengers sailed her on her long, luxurious trips. We gave extraordinary service—600 passengers being looked after by 600 staff. But mostly, we had 300 or 400 passengers.

"In still-rationed Britain, the *Caronia* also had the best food—the finest meats, the finest wines, and even the finest caviar, which was served in large silver bowls. I'd run errands for the passengers, mostly lots of elderly couples and, more so, lots of elderly, single ladies. Sometimes I just spent time chatting with them. And sometimes, I was given $50–100 tips, which were, well, like a thousand dollars in the late '40s. But the best payment was to travel the world aboard a ship such as the luxurious *Caronia*. Here was a simple, young boy from a little English town who was visiting New York and the likes of Barbados, Rio de Janeiro, and Capetown. Yes, wonderful memories."

The *Caronia* arriving at Pier 90, New York. (*ALF Collection*)

26

The Great *Norway*: Cato Christensen

Cato Christensen was staff captain, between 1999 and 2001, of one of the greatest ocean liners of all time: the *Norway*. She was the world's first mega-cruise liner, the longest passenger ship afloat for many years, and was, of course, the illustrious *France* in her previous life. As Captain Christensen and I sat together in the warm, blue waters of the Eastern Caribbean, aboard the *Crystal Symphony*, we recalled the great *Norway*. Her last remains had been chopped up by scrappers out in India just the month before, in October 2008. The *Norway* had been around for forty-three years, since her initial commissioning as the pride of the French merchant marine in late 1961.

"As the *Norway*, she still had this great ambience. It was very special. She had a different feeling than other ships," recalled the captain. "There was history, even great history, in the walls. Even in some of her public rooms, such as the Club International, there was a special tone. Simply, she was like no other ship."

Built at St. Nazaire in western France for the final years, the twilight, of the great and grand North Atlantic run, the ship as the *France* carried 2,000 passengers—500 in fancy, upper-deck first class and 1,500 in tourist class. She had vast public rooms, an array of luxurious penthouses and suites, a chapel, and dog kennels complete with miniature New York City fire hydrants.

Her food was often said to be beyond compare and was coupled with the finest wine cellar at sea; even the dogs had menus, and the dog biscuits were specially made.

She sailed for about nine months of the year on regular relays between Manhattan's Pier 88, Southampton, and Le Havre; for the rest, she cruised to the Caribbean, the Mediterranean, Carnival in Rio. In 1972 and '74, she also made winter cruises around the world.

But, as passengers declined, her operational costs rose and while the French government pulled the plug on her operating subsidy, the *France* was decommissioned in October 1974. For almost five years, she sat idle, at a backwater berth near Le Havre, and just waited. She might even have been scrapped.

But Norwegian Cruise Lines bought her in August 1979, then gave her a costly $150 million makeover as a cruise ship, and afterward introduced her as the *Norway* in May 1990. Her new role: weekly seven-night cruises from Miami to sun-filled ports in the Eastern Caribbean.

"The *Norway* was strong and solid, and built like very few other ships," added Captain Christensen. "Her watertight doors, for example, could be individually operated and closed in thirty seconds. They were so advanced for a ship designed in the '50s and built in the early '60s. Although the forward engine room had been removed by NCL, she had her original steam turbines. But I think Kloster [then the owner of NCL] regretted not converting her to diesel during the big refit in 1979–80. She was, of course, quite a different ship to handle and to experience. She had delayed maneuvers. There were forty-five-second delays. It was always quite an experience to handle this 1,035-foot-long ship in, say, the Miami turning basin."

"But she was a great ship to the end," continued the captain. "Of course, we needed extra staff in the engine room because of those steam turbines. The crew mostly loved her. They felt, quite rightfully, that she was a ship of history. They worked extra hard to make her work. We had one man continuously painting, for example, in the galley just to keep it looking spotless and fresh. About 85–90 percent of the crew always returned to her. Her U.S. Public Health Scores were sometimes on the edge because of her age, and we'd always lose two points just because of that. Most of Deck 5 was still original, for example, and so were many of the suites. In the captain's office, there was still a button on the desk that connected directly to the pantry for instant service. As vice-captain, my cabin had been the 'dog house' when the ship had a large kennel. The kennels themselves and that New York City fire hydrant were gone, however. By 2001, we still had great passenger loads and lots of repeater passengers. One guest came with his butler and had a big suite for four to six cruises at a time. But once the butler sent the chauffeur and the car off, but with all the luggage as well. So, the chauffeur had to fly to the first port of call, to St Thomas, with the luggage and the clothes."

The *Norway* had a serious boiler explosion at her Miami berth in May 2003. Six crew members were killed, and others seriously injured. "NCL lost almost all interest in her after the explosion," concluded Captain Christensen. "Star Cruises, the new Malaysian parent of NCL, lost interest as well. Everything actually changed with Star. The mood was different. There was no chance of seeing her getting expensive repairs and returning to service. Of course, now it is very sad that she has been scrapped. She should have been saved, possibly as a museum and hotel, and like the *QE2* in Dubai. This would have been better. Her steel hull was still so strong. It was 2 inches thick below the waterline. We once had a problem undocking. Bit in the end, there was more damage to the pier than to the ship."

The newly refitted *Norway* arriving at New York in May 1980. (*Author's Collection*)

27
Indian Ocean Sailing: David Andrews

When David Andrews joined the British India Steam Navigation Company Limited, "BI" as it was abbreviated, in 1954, the British Merchant Navy had some 6,000 ships and employed as many as 50,000 seamen. Trade was brisk almost everywhere in the world and the British Empire, though in its own Indian summer, was largely intact. Alone, BI had 136 ships. For Andrews, it was a career that went from freighters to passenger ships and finally to super tankers.

"My first ship was the freighter *Chantala*, which was also the Company's training ship," he recalled. "She carried up to forty cadets plus forty-four regular crew and twelve passengers. Altogether there was close to 100 on board. We were on BI's U.K.–Australia service. Later, I went to BI's O Class freighters, which sailed between Bombay and Karachi and then to Malaysia, Hong Kong, and Japan. In some areas, we were still on alert for mines left over from World War II. We carried all sorts of cargo—such as dates and cotton and even scrap metal from India to the Far East, and then returned with items such as sulfur, carbon, even sugar and newspaper."

British India was an empire of sorts in itself. There were large company offices in Bombay, Calcutta, Singapore, Hong Kong, Mombasa, and the main headquarters in London. We had British managers and either Indian or Chinese clerks in the overseas offices.

Even by 1960, British India had ten passenger ships. Andrews served on many of them. "I was assigned to the little *Daressa*, [5,000 tons and over 1,000 passengers], which was used on the Bombay–Persian Gulf service. Our big trade was Indians traveling as deck class. Next, it was to the *Sangola* [8,600 tons and 500 passengers], which was on the run between India, Southeast Asia, and the Far East. It was a long-haul service extending from Bombay all the way to Kobe and Yokohama. Again, we carried some passengers in first class, but mostly Chinese down in deck class."

One of Andrews' favorite assignments was sailing between India, the Seychelles, and then ports in East and South Africa on board the popular sister ships *Karanja* and *Kampala* (10,300 tons, 1,000 passengers). "We'd carry South African passengers, businessmen, and even tourists in first class and Indian workers in deck class. The South Africans often used these ships for their holidays—sailing from Durban up to Mombasa, then spend time ashore in a hotel and then catch the returning ship back to Durban. The *Karanja*

and *Kampala* worked on four-week roundtrip schedules. They were lovely ships for both passengers and for crew. They weren't air-conditioned, but we were soon used to the heat and also had big fans in our cabins. As officers, we were expected to learn Hindi and always carried a language book."

David's next assignment was to the sisters *Amra* and *Aronda* (8,300 tons, 1,100 passengers). Each ship sailed on a different service. "The *Amra* sailed between Karachi and Mombasa whereas the *Aronda* went around India, sailing between East and West Pakistan, between Chittagong and Karachi. Mostly, the Pakistani passengers were kept separate from the Indian passengers. These ships were very fast and, like most other BI ships of that time, were well built and heavily riveted.

"The very best assignments at BI were the little passenger ship *Mombasa* [2,200 tons, 275 passengers], which sailed only along the East African coast between Mombasa and Mtwara. She was often back in Mombasa, where many BI officers had wives and families. The other was the BI tugboat *Alusha*, which towed BI's barges along the East African coast."

David did not return to his home in England for several years at a time. "We worked on three-year contracts and then had leave and could go home for six months. We caught BI freighters going to and from the U.K. But BI was like a big family. There was a BI Club in each port and these included sleeping accommodations. There were even ship-like restaurants in these clubs and the officers sat at the head tables and the juniors elsewhere. These were busy places, especially since there were always four or five British India ships in port."

But times were changing. Decolonization of British territories moved quickly by the early 1960s and almost immediately changed trading patterns for British flag ships, passenger as well as freight. Then the huge P&O Company, owners of British India, took a stronger hold and decided to gradually phase-out the BI passenger division. And finally, British seamen were becoming more expensive by the 1960s. Everything, it seemed, was changing. British India itself slowly downsized and all but disappeared completely by the mid-1980s. David Andrews, by now a captain, decided to make a change—he joined P&O-owned Trident Tankers. From the likes of the 2,200-ton *Mombasa* and the 1,000-passenger *Karanja*, he was now in command of giant 200,000-ton tankers.

British India Line's *Karanja* loading at Bombay. (*Author's Collection*)

Later in their careers, British India passenger ships were repainted in all-white. (*British India Line*)

Together at Mombasa: P&O's *Cathay* (left) and the *Karanja* are in port. (*P&O*)

The *Karanja* could accommodate upwards of 1,100 passengers—in a smallish first and second class, but a substantial third class. (*Mick Lindsay Collection*)

Above: Another view of the 1947-built *Karanja* at Mombasa. (*British India Line*)

Right: An alternate service was the so-called Bay of Bengal route. (*Author's Collection*)

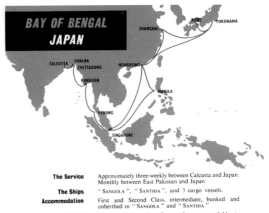

The Service	Approximately three-weekly between Calcutta and Japan. Monthly between East Pakistan and Japan
The Ships	" SANGOLA ", " SANTHIA ", and 3 cargo vessels.
Accommodation	First and Second Class, intermediate, bunked and unberthed in " SANGOLA " and " SANTHIA "
Freight	General cargo with refrigerated space available in " SANGOLA " and " SANTHIA "
Ports of Call	Calcutta, East Pakistan, Burma, Malaya, Hong Kong and Japan, calling at Manila and other intermediate ports as required. Cargo vessels call Shanghai inwards to India.
Schedule	Calcutta to Japan—26 days.

The 8,600-ton *Santhia* was on the run between Calcutta, Singapore, Hong Kong, and Japan. (*British India Line*)

The smallish 5,000-ton *Daressa* and her three sisters were used on the Persian Gulf run out of Bombay. (*British India Line*)

Above left: The *Dwarka*, seen at Bombay, endured until the early 1980s. (*British India Line*)

Above right: Another view of the long-lasting *Dwarka* at Bombay. (*British India Line*)

The little 2,200-grt *Mombasa* was used on the local East African coast run out of Mombasa. (*British India Line*)

28

High Luxury on the High Seas: Nick Evans

Growing-up near Southampton, Nick Evans was just twenty-one years old when he joined Royal Mail Lines' 500-passenger *Andes* in 1963 as a junior radio officer. She was then one of the most luxurious cruise liners afloat and did little else other than three- and four-week cruises from Southampton.

"I knew that she was a famous ship, well known in and around the port of Southampton, and on board she seemed to me to be like an old, luxurious hotel. Everything was polished woods, softly lighted and altogether gleaming," recalled Nick. "We cruised to places like the Mediterranean and Norway. But occasionally we had our incidents. I remember lines twisting onto one of the ship's propellers at Lisbon and also having a small fire at Corfu. The passengers were all older and very formal, at least to a ywenty-one-year-old like me. We had, as I remember, very, very few young passengers except possibly the grandchildren of grandparent-passengers. But looking back, I don't think I fully appreciated the experience of serving and sailing on a ship such as the *Andes*. I stayed with her for thirteen months, but then joined the Royal Naval Fleet Auxiliary."

The classic *Andes* was one of Britain's most popular cruise ships. (*Author's Collection*)

29
Popular P&O Liner: Henry Poulton

Long retired, Henry Poulton spent twenty years, beginning in 1957, with the illustrious P&O Lines. He sailed mostly as a dining room waiter and mostly aboard the 29,000-ton, 1,500-passenger *Arcadia.*

"The *Arcadia* was a great ship, perhaps my favorite at P&O, and had a friendly on-board feeling about her," he remembered. "We sailed about nine months of the year on the U.K.–Australia run, down to Fremantle, Melbourne, and Sydney. We usually went out by way of the Suez Canal, but sometimes went completely around-the-world as a return, using the Panama route as a return. Up in first class, we had lots of elegant, posh passengers—businessmen, government people, up-market tourists. But down in tourist, it was a different story, much like another world. We carried lots and lots of 'Ten Pound Poms,' very simple British families going out to Australia to resettle.

Many of them were very poor and some had never been served a meal in their entire lives. They were sometimes very short on manners, rarely tipped and had a sense of fear in heading off to that unknown land Down Under.

"Sometimes, in tourist class, we'd have several hundred children aboard but many could be quite unruly and misbehaved. They often turned tourist class into a playground and sometimes even tried their hand at slipping into first class. Then for the remaining three months of the year, the *Arcadia* would go cruising, but two classes in those days, from Southampton and sometimes from Sydney. The British cruise passengers tended to be older and even gentile whereas the Australians were younger, loud, and noisy—and they wanted to party day after day. So, in the course of a year, a ship like the *Arcadia* had many different types of passengers—and so many different moods."

The 721-foot-long *Arcadia* at Melbourne.
(*Tim Noble Collection*)

Above: Outbound off Southampton, the *Arcadia* and her near-sister *Iberia* depart simultaneously. (*P&O*)

Below left: South Pacific sailing on board the *Arcadia*. (*Kay Stephens*)

Below right: The *Arcadia* arrives at Sydney. (*ALF Collection*)

Imposing: The 29,734-ton *Arcadia* off Gravesend, London. (*Mick Lindsay Collection*)

Fond farewell: The last visit to Melbourne for the *Arcadia* in 1979. Sitmar's *Fairstar* is on the left. (*Tim Noble Collection*)

Above: Bon voyage to the 1,410-passenger *Arcadia*. (*Tim Noble Collection*)

Below left: Cruising on P&O. (*Author's Collection*)

Below right: An interesting P&O baggage tag. (*Author's Collection*)

30
Peacetime Trooping: Robert Stanhope

Robert Stanhope joined P&O in the early 1950s and stayed with the famous shipping line for the next forty-one years. He began on a British government peacetime troopship, the *Empire Fowey*, that was managed by P&O and so carried P&O officers, crew, and even the traditional Lascars on deck. A 17,000-tonner, she had been a German liner of the 1930s, the *Potsdam*, used on the Hamburg–Far East run, but then seized by the British when World War II ended in 1945. As a trooper, she carried up to 1,600 government passengers in four classes.

"We were carrying full loads of troops during the Malaysian wars when I was aboard," remembered Robert. "The troops and crew like me lived in eight- to ten-bunk cabins down on the lowest decks. The voyages were long and of course very warm, sometimes boiling, but we had wind scoops for the portholes and so we adjusted to the cool sea air. There was nothing like air conditioning in those days, of course. Coming back to the U.K. from Singapore and Penang, we carried British families and the British children that were evacuated from the war-torn areas. We also had returning soldiers and lots of wounded. The hospital aboard the *Empire Fowey* was top-flight, as good as any hospital, say, ashore in London."

"Once, we were ordered to do a thorough cleaning of the *Empire Fowey*," concluded Robert. "I was assigned to the oak-lined main foyer. When we lifted off the portrait of the queen for cleaning, we found something underneath—the mounting for a Nazi eagle and swastika."

The British troopship *Empire Fowey*. (*Author's Collection*)

31

Henderson Line to Rangoon: George Munn

George Munn had served for six years, beginning in the mid-1950s, aboard the tankers of BP—British Petroleum. But he needed a change and in 1961 joined the Glasgow-based Henderson Line, a now largely forgotten, smallish shipping firm that traded between the U.K. and distant Burma. He was soon assigned, as second engineer, to the Henderson freighter *Bhamo*.

"She made three-month roundtrips beginning at Glasgow and then Liverpool (Birkenhead) and then to Amsterdam, Genoa, Suez, Aden, Colombo, and finally Rangoon," recalled George. "We'd have three weeks in Rangoon offloading and then loading for the return voyage. We made four round trips a year. Outbound, we carried just about everything—all sorts of British manufactured goods. Homeward, we carried cotton, jute, and rubber."

There was a close call on one return voyage aboard the *Bhamo*. "On a return voyage, we had a nasty fire while loading cargo at Port Said," said George. "Local dockers had been smoking down in the hold. Smoke soon filled the hatch. We closed the hatch and the fire continued to smolder as we sailed onward to Genoa. The heat caused some of the upper deck areas to buckle, but was finally fully extinguished days later at Genoa. But when we finally reached Liverpool, the British dockers wanted more money for handling fire-damaged cargo."

Artist Stephen Card's interesting painting of Henderson Line's *Pegu*. (*Stephen Card Collection*)

32

Final Days of the *Queen Elizabeth/Seawise University*: Arthur Taylor

Arthur Taylor worked in a different aspect of shipping—but mostly marine financing. "Mainly, in the 1960s and '70s, I was involved in the financing by Taiwanese scrap metal companies to buy old ships," he recalled. "A twenty-five-year-old, 7,100-ton Liberty ship, for example, then [in 1970] changed hands for about $125,000. I also dealt with many T-2 Tankers that had been built in the U.S. in the mid-1940s. Some deals failed, of course. But I had one Chinese client who wanted to buy a big ship: the giant *Queen Elizabeth*, which was being auctioned-off at Fort Lauderdale in 1970. He wanted it for scrapping. But he didn't have all the monies needed. So his plan was to raise money by selling pieces of the ship's two funnels, each a square-inch and placed in a plexiglass block. He would sell them, so he thought, all over the world. But nothing ever came of this plan."

Based in Hong Kong, British-born Arthur did lots of work with many of the great Chinese shipping tycoons, namely C. Y. Tung and Y. K. Pao. They bought lots of older, secondhand ships as well as built brand-new ones. "Tung especially was a very interesting man. He began by owning a wheelbarrow and used along the docks," added Taylor. "He was hugely ambitious, worked very hard and soon bought a small tanker. Eventually, he amassed [in the 1970s] one of the largest fleets in the world [namely, the Orient Overseas Line], which included passenger ships such as the *Queen Elizabeth*, *Independence*, and *Constitution*. But stories to this day of him sabotaging the former *Queen Elizabeth* [renamed *Seawise University*] in 1972 for insurance reasons are totally untrue. He was very proud of buying that famous former Cunard liner. Later, when visiting him at his townhouse in London and where he had his own movie theater, he showed films of the *Queen Elizabeth*, his other passenger ships and even his freighters and tankers. As we sat back and watched, he silently beamed with pride."

"And Y. K. Pao, also interested in tankers and bulk carriers but not passenger ships, was said to be one of the richest men in the world by the late 1970s. He was a multi-billionaire," concluded Arthur Taylor. "He once said that it would cost him about a $1 million just to stop and figure out how much he was totally worth."

Ravaged by fire and capsized in Hong Kong harbor, the sad remains of the *Seawise University*, the former *Queen Elizabeth*. (*Author's Collection*)

33

Greek Cruising: Terry Hopley

Terry Hopley has had a very interesting life with ships— and, overall, a very diverse life. He had been in naval intelligence, then a sports journalist for a newspaper, a tour operator, a ship's commodore, an author as well as publisher and, most recently, a dance host aboard none other than the *Queen Mary 2*. Expectedly, he is gifted with a charming, very outgoing personality—and blessed, as he said, "with the gift of the gab."

Born to a poor family in London, he certainly went on to create a diversely rich and colorful life. After doing naval intelligence with Britain's Royal Navy, he began the first of several reinventions of himself—first becoming a sportswriter and eventually writing for eighteen different newspapers. "Back in the early 1970s, I was invited to dinner aboard the *Black Watch* [9,600 tons] of the Fred Olsen Line," he said. "In the winter, that ship was carrying British tourists, 400–500 passengers, on two-week cruises to the sunny Canary Islands. On the return, it carried loads of tomatoes as well. Suddenly, I became interested in cruising. I soon decided I could book my sports page readers on cruises and so I chartered the *Black Watch* as well as her sister ship, the *Black Prince*, and then the bigger *Blenheim*. I accompanied the trips and, spending much time on the bridge, also began to take an interest in navigation. Soon, between cruises, I was taking shoreside navigation courses."

The travel industry, especially cruising, appealed more and more to Terry. He later bought Four Winds Cruises, then one of the U.K.'s biggest cruise ship charterers. He did lots of business with Gerry Herrod, a cruise legend of sorts, who was then running Ocean Cruise Lines with three ships—the *Ocean Princess*, *Ocean Islander*, and, out in the Far East, *Ocean Pearl*. Herrod's operations were all but ruined, however, by the near-sinking in the Amazon of the *Ocean Princess* in March 1993. However, he later went on to buy Russia's *Alexandr Pushkin*, rebuild it as the *Marco Polo*, and start-up a new company, the Orient Line. When he later sold that ship and company, he created yet another cruise line. Terry added, "He kept reinventing himself and his business. Now, he was running the *Aegean Dolphin*, a converted ferry but that ran like a 'crab.' She was a terrible ship—she always turned the wrong way! Persistent, he later started Voyages to Antiquity and refitted that old ship as the 'new' *Aegean Odyssey*."

Afterward, Terry himself teamed up with investor James Sherwood, who bought the famed Orient Express. The train was unable to travel between London and Istanbul, however, and so Sherwood bought a passenger ship, aptly named the *Orient Express*, for connecting services—the train from London to Venice and then the ship from Venice to Istanbul.

Then it was on to the Greeks. Terry met George Louris, a Greek shipowner who ran the converted, 10,000-ton cruise ship *La Perla*. "She had been a French ship, the *Ferdinand des Lesseps*, that carried passengers in about four classes out to East Africa and Indian Ocean ports. Louris rebuilt her for Mediterranean cruising. Unfortunately, she had all sorts of problems in the beginning— being 'arrested' for unpaid bills, poor on-board conditions and sometimes having more rats aboard than passengers. Louris refitted the ship, reinvented his cruise business, and then reintroduced her as the *La Palma*. He appointed me 'commodore'. He paid me 1,000 pounds a week—and for ten years! He liked me. A 'real' captain was hired to run the ship, but I had full power, second only to Louris himself. I wore full dress whites complete with gold buttons. George Louris was a true Greek ship owner— wearing the best suits, diamond cufflinks, smoking expensive cigars. Sometimes we'd have meetings at the fancy Savoy Grill in London. On board the ship, he kept an owner's suite just for himself. Business was good for a time and we were actually thinking of expanding and almost bought a second ship, the Portugese *Funchal*."

Terry left cruising for some years and moved to Australia (sailing out aboard Costa's *Danae*). Later, while he consulted on the building of a cruise terminal at Brisbane (and gradually took on an Australian accent), he realised he missed ships and the sea. After returning to England, he formed a publishing company and returned to journalism, which included writing cruise reviews. "But I really wanted to go back to sea," he concluded. "I actually admired, even envied dance hosts and so, at age seventy, I went to dancing school. I danced for six hours a day, then went to an agency and was sent off on my first cruise. I loved it. So here I am, dancing in the Queen's Room aboard the last Atlantic liner, the *Queen Mary 2*."

Right: The sleek cruise ship *Italia*, seen at Tenerife in 1983. (*Author's Collection*)

Below left: Eastern Mediterranean cruising on board the *La Palma*. (*Author's Collection*)

Below right: Printed material for the *La Palma*. (*Andrew Kilk Collection*)

1993

La Palma

ITALY · GREECE · TURKEY

INTERCRUISE LTD.

THE ITINERARY DAY BY DAY

Voyage	1	2	3	4	5	6	7	8	9	10	11	12	13	14	15	16	17	18	19	20	21	22	23	24
VENICE Sat. dep. 13.00h	Apr. 24	May 01	May 08	May 15	May 22	May 29	Jun. 05	Jun. 12	Jun. 19	Jun. 26	Jul. 03	Jul. 10	Jul. 17	Jul. 24	Jul. 31	Aug. 07	Aug. 14	Aug. 21	Aug. 28	Sep. 04	Sep. 11	Sep. 18	Sep. 25	Oct. 02
CORFU Sun. 19.00-22.00h	Apr. 25	May 02	May 09	May 16	May 23	May 30	Jun. 06	Jun. 13	Jun. 20	Jun. 27	Jul. 04	Jul. 11	Jul. 18	Jul. 25	Aug. 01	Aug. 08	Aug. 15	Aug. 22	Aug. 29	Sep. 05	Sep. 12	Sep. 19	Sep. 26	Oct. 03
PIRAEUS Mon. 15.00-20.00h	Apr. 26	May 03	May 10	May 17	May 24	May 31	Jun. 07	Jun. 14	Jun. 21	Jun. 28	Jul. 05	Jul. 12	Jul. 19	Jul. 26	Aug. 02	Aug. 09	Aug. 16	Aug. 23	Aug. 30	Sep. 06	Sep. 13	Sep. 20	Sep. 27	Oct. 04
KUSADASI Tue. 06.00-12.00h	Apr. 27	May 04	May 11	May 18	May 25	Jun. 01	Jun. 08	Jun. 15	Jun. 22	Jun. 29	Jul. 06	Jul. 13	Jul. 20	Jul. 27	Aug. 03	Aug. 10	Aug. 17	Aug. 24	Aug. 31	Sep. 07	Sep. 14	Sep. 21	Sep. 28	Oct. 05
PATMOS Tue. 16.00-21.00h	Apr. 27	May 04	May 11	May 18	May 25	Jun. 01	Jun. 08	Jun. 15	Jun. 22	Jun. 29	Jul. 06	Jul. 13	Jul. 20	Jul. 27	Aug. 03	Aug. 10	Aug. 17	Aug. 24	Aug. 31	Sep. 07	Sep. 14	Sep. 21	Sep. 28	Oct. 05
RHODES Wed. 07.00-12.00h	Apr. 28	May 05	May 12	May 19	May 26	Jun. 02	Jun. 09	Jun. 16	Jun. 23	Jun. 30	Jul. 07	Jul. 14	Jul. 21	Jul. 28	Aug. 04	Aug. 11	Aug. 18	Aug. 25	Sep. 01	Sep. 08	Sep. 15	Sep. 22	Sep. 29	Oct. 06
KATAKOLON/OLYMPIA Thu. 13.00-17.30h	Apr. 29	May 06	May 13	May 20	May 27	Jun. 03	Jun. 10	Jun. 17	Jun. 24	Jul. 01	Jul. 08	Jul. 15	Jul. 22	Jul. 29	Aug. 05	Aug. 12	Aug. 19	Aug. 26	Sep. 02	Sep. 09	Sep. 16	Sep. 23	Sep. 30	Oct. 07
AT SEA Friday	Apr. 30	May 07	May 14	May 21	May 28	Jun. 04	Jun. 11	Jun. 18	Jun. 25	Jul. 02	Jul. 09	Jul. 16	Jul. 23	Jul. 30	Aug. 06	Aug. 13	Aug. 20	Aug. 27	Sep. 03	Sep. 10	Sep. 17	Sep. 24	Oct. 01	Oct. 08
VENICE Sat. arr. 08.00h	May 01	May 08	May 15	May 22	May 29	Jun. 05	Jun. 12	Jun. 19	Jun. 26	Jul. 03	Jul. 10	Jul. 17	Jul. 24	Jul. 31	Aug. 07	Aug. 14	Aug. 21	Aug. 28	Sep. 04	Sep. 11	Sep. 18	Sep. 25	Oct. 02	Oct. 09

DECK PLAN LA PALMA

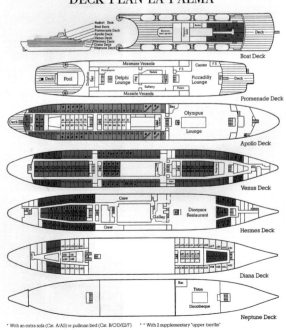

* With an extra sofa (Cat. A/AS) or pullman bed (Cat. B/C/D/E2/F)   * * With 2 supplementary 'upper-berths'

34

To the Age of Pandemic & COVID: Scott Peterson

I n November 2021, while cruising from Miami to the Bahamas on the ever-splendid *Crystal Serenity*, I interviewed my old friend Scott Peterson, the ship's hotel director. The topic: the COVID lockdown for cruise ships.

It was one of the worst periods in cruising history—COVID swept around the world and travel, including cruising, ground to an almost screeching halt. Then business stopped for sixteen months; in some places even longer. Indeed, they were disruptive, financially crippling, and very tense times. Overall, the big U.S. cruise lines were losing an estimated $287,000 a day—or something like $17,000 a minute.

Scott Peterson saw much of the cruising COVID shutdown. "We were in Auckland, New Zealand, in February 2020 and suddenly we saw the escalation of COVID," he recalled. "We had to make sudden and very serious decisions. The guests were finally sent home in a matter of weeks, from Perth in Australia, and the world cruise was officially canceled.

"The *Serenity* then 'deadheaded' to Singapore. We had 400-plus crew on board. We had two weeks at anchor in quarantine before being allowed into Singapore. Then Singapore was closed and we moved to Port Klang in Malaysia. From there, we tried to get some of 400 crew home—the South Africans, the Indians, the Filipinos. Later, we took on some crew from our sister vessel, the *Crystal Symphony*, and from other Genting-owned cruise ships [Genting Hong Kong then owned Crystal as well as Asian-based Star Cruises and Dream Cruises]. We sailed for Manila, but each crew member had be isolated in a cabin, one to a room, for fourteen days to be admitted under Philippines restrictions. The crew were no longer being paid, but we did our best to care for them. Even the officers took a voluntary reduction in pay. We delivered three meals a day to each crew cabin—and everyone else helped. It was a huge team work effort, the true Crystal team spirit. Once anchored in Manila harbor, then the crew had to face local quarantine on shore. There were lots of hoops!

"We returned to Port Klang with 200 crewmembers and then they were slowly sent home, but with great difficulties. Places such as South Africa, India, and others were tightly closed. Myself, I spent 111 days on board the ship without stepping ashore.

"For those crew still on board, we tried to make it comfortable. We had lots of food, free Internet and even ran barbecues on deck. The ship was 100 percent safe. The crew were housed in crew quarters, but also guest rooms. The air-conditioning had to be reduced to lessen fuel, the ship was very warm in some areas and much of the ship was quite dark. Areas like Prego, Umi Uma, and the Stardust Lounge were shut down. We also had to deal with leaks, bugs, and mold. The reduced air-conditioning in those very, very hot and humid waters created mold. By November, we were down to minimum manning of sixty-one officers and crew—approximately twenty each from the hotel, deck, and engine departments. Of course, everyone still had to be fed and kept clean and safe. But everyone pulled together. Once, we went to Batan in Indonesia for a crew change. We were together and on board for Christmas, and everyone was given a small gift. We had a Christmas dinner and then a barbecue on deck for New Year's Eve. Fortunately, morale remained high.

"The ship itself was eerie at times, even lonely. Even the exterior of the ship began to look very scruffy. There was tremendous growth on the hull. Finally, in early May [2021], we left Port Klang and went to Singapore for drydocking. Then we sailed to the Suez Canal and up to the Mediterranean. At Limassol [Cyprus], we took on more and more crew. Fortunately, we had internet and phone communication, but limited TV. Myself, I kept fit by walking the terrace of my stateroom forty-five times twice a day. Next, we had further drydocking, cleaning and refitting at Cadiz [Spain]."

Scott concluded, "Finally, it was time to resume regular service. In June, we sailed to the Bahamas, which took ten days and on a perfect, glass-like sea all the way. Fortunately, we are a Bahamas-registered ship and so the country opened up to us—with mandatory onboard and operational protocols, of course. Our first cruise, on July 3 (seven days from Nassau around the Bahamas), had 600 passengers. We added Miami stops starting in August—and so we could offer cruises from Nassau and Bimini as well as Miami. We were back in business—and everyone here on board is very happy and very grateful!"

The luxurious *Crystal Serenity* seen in Norwegian waters in July 2003. (*Author's Collection*)

The *Crystal Serenity* seen in the Bahamas in November 2021. (*Author's Collection*)

Bibliography

Dunn, L., *Passenger Liners* (Southampton, England: Adlard Coles Ltd., 1961)

Miller, W. H., *Pictorial Encyclopedia of Ocean Liners 1860–1994* (Mineola, New York: Dover Publications Inc., 1995)